Narratives and Strategies for Promoting Indigenous Education

T0299788

This book describes the experiences of students, educators, and community members living in the Zuni Pueblo and working to integrate Indigenous language, culture, and history in in the Zuni Pueblo schools. Aimed at teacher education faculty seeking to work in collaborative relationships with Indigenous populations, this volume offers a first-hand account of the challenges and opportunities surrounding the preservation of Indigenous culture in pre-K-12 curriculum and instruction. Featuring a range of perspectives from within a tribal educational institution, this book demonstrates the possibilities for successful partnerships between Indigenous schools and Western systems of education.

Cheryl A. Torrez is a professor in the Department of Teacher Education, Educational Leadership and Policy at the University of New Mexico, USA.

Marjori Krebs is an associate professor in the Department of Teacher Education, Educational Leadership and Policy at the University of New Mexico, USA.

Narratives and Strategies for Promoting Indigenous Education

Empowering Teachers and Community in the Zuni Pueblo

**Edited by
Marjori Krebs
Cheryl A. Torrez**

Routledge
Taylor & Francis Group

LONDON AND NEW YORK

First published 2019
by Routledge

2 Park Square, Milton Park, Abingdon, Oxfordshire OX14 4RN
52 Vanderbilt Avenue, New York, NY 10017

*Routledge is an imprint of the Taylor & Francis Group,
an informa business*

First issued in paperback 2020

Library of Congress Cataloguing-in-Publication Data
A catalog record for this book has been requested

ISBN: 978-1-138-48000-1 (hbk)
ISBN: 978-0-367-60689-3 (pbk)

Typeset in Times New Roman
by Apex CoVantage, LLC

Contents

Foreword: Strengthening and Maintaining Indigenous Culture: Integrating Zuni Language, Culture, and History in the Educational Systems Serving the Zuni Community

Indigenous tribal populations in the United States and throughout the world have continued the struggle to strengthen identity, maintain cultural practices, and create proactive solutions to address cultural and community needs. Every Indigenous population on earth has been impacted to some degree by the *great interruption*. By this I refer to the imposition of European forms of colonization and colonial expansion among Indigenous tribal populations.

In the United States, the colonizing process, which still continues in different forms, has had a devastating impact upon the lives of Indigenous people because of warfare, intentional genocide, dispossession of lands, destruction of culturally significant lands and places of worship, confiscation and warehousing of culturally important artifacts, devaluing of languages and spiritual practices through the introduction of foreign religions and education systems, and the forced physical separation of children from their natural families and homelands. Obviously, the list of atrocities may easily extend to other areas beyond the partial list of impacts referenced above. The impacts of colonization have resulted in serious challenges for Indigenous peoples as we collectively and individually work to restore and strengthen hope, reestablish or strengthen tribal identity to restore, strengthen, or reestablish the sacred history, practices, and languages that are an integral aspect of our lives, culture, and lineage as Indigenous people.

We continue to decolonize ourselves and our communities using a variety of techniques and resources. In "developed" nations, the tools, resources, experiences, methods of research, and writing of ways to overcome such challenges are often viewed as the rightful realm of university-trained scholars and academics who understand the theoretical and intellectual implications of the colonizing process. However, we (reservation-based Indigenous) see ourselves as the ones who are on the line daily, living and working in small, but significant ways to overcome the entrenched and systemic structures of colonization that are found in the imposed systems of education serving tribal communities. These include: public PK-12 schools, higher education, public charter schools, Bureau of Indian Affairs/Bureau of Indian Education (BIA/BIE) contract-grant schools, and religious-based schools. These are all *closed* systems of education designed and implemented by the colonizer nations to be literally impervious to change. Tribes have had little influence to change the structure, policies, teaching practices, or content over time. In many cases the only change has been the appointment or election of Indian boards of education, administrators, some teachers, and many non-licensed Indigenous support staff. However, many Indigenous people charged with the responsibility to govern these systems have not bothered to change the governance or implementing structures, curriculum, policies, and teaching practices which form the backbone of these neo-colonizing institutions found on many reservations in the United States.

In Zuni, we have an opportunity to change the PK-12 and higher education systems serving the tribal community. The process of preparing for this change will necessarily mean the reclaiming of our voices, making proactive and life-enhancing choices, and reclaiming the power to heal ourselves and our community in proactive, appropriate, and sustainable ways. The ingredients for this change are evident and are represented by the chapters included in this book.

The first-person accounts of the writers provide important insights of current educational practices as well as the ways they envision to strengthen the integration of Zuni language, culture, and history into the curriculum of the schools in Zuni. The Zuni Public School District (ZPSD) was created with the express intent by tribal leaders to include a bilingual/bicultural curriculum to focus on creating Zuni language learning, maintenance, and cultural studies as an essential aspect of the educational service for all students. At this point, there exists no coherent policy or comprehensive curriculum to include Zuni language, culture, and history for PK-12 students in any systemic manner. If clear and culturally supportive policies regarding Zuni language and cultural integration are not ratified by the ZPSD school board and implemented by district administrators, then Zuni language classes, cultural studies, and history will continue to be relegated to an afterthought.

This book contains the voices of community people supported by *Zuni: Engaging Teachers and Community*. This grant, funded by the W.K. Kellogg Foundation, has been a partnership between the tribe of Zuni, the University of New Mexico, and the ZPSD. The authors are challenged daily by the colonizing structures of schools that promote status quo maintenance of the systems. Their experiences, as described in their narratives, are important lessons of *what is,* and the descriptions of *what is* have the distinct possibility of leading to a position of *what can be*, which entails creating a stronger tribal definition of what education should be and how such systems may serve to strengthen tribal language, culture, and community development opportunities by using the resources of cultural and ancestral knowledge and teaching practices that are culturally responsive and supportive.

We are grateful for the research and writing represented by our community members as these are important examples of their current educational work, lived experiences, and aspirations. The stories, experiences, thoughts, and recommendations of the authors are an essential step in this process of reclaiming and redefining a culturally appropriate education for Zuni citizens.

We look forward to continuing in partnership and with enlightened choices as we undertake the responsibility of redesigning the PK-12 and higher education systems serving our community, children, youth, and adults.

Hayes A. Lewis
A:shiwi College & Career Readiness Center
Pueblo of Zuni

Preface

Marjori Krebs and Cheryl A. Torrez

We compiled the chapters in this book so the stories of our partners could be told to a larger audience. As editors, we are two teacher preparation faculty members at the University of New Mexico in the College of Education. We began our work with members of the Zuni Pueblo in 2013, as partners in a grant from the W. K. Kellogg Foundation. The primary goal of this grant (Zuni: Engaging Teachers and Community—ZETAC) was to increase the number of Zuni tribal members who teach in the Zuni Pueblo. To do this, we needed to recruit, advise, and admit Zuni members to our teacher preparation programs and support them in obtaining their degrees and teaching licenses from the state of New Mexico.

In addition, through professional development sessions, ZETAC sought to

a) provide a social and cultural orientation for current and future teachers,
b) reestablish a sense of empowerment among principals and teachers,
c) facilitate collegial and collaborative work across the district,
d) recruit current Indigenous students to become teachers, and
e) provide educational opportunities through scholarship dollars for teachers and future teachers to obtain graduate and undergraduate degrees.

The majority of participants attended professional development workshops focused on Zuni history, culture, and language, and incorporating Project-Based Learning (PBL) into their teaching. Over the course of five years, we have conducted numerous professional development sessions lasting between one to five days, depending on the topic and the time of year. The chapters you will read share the highlights of both the authors' experiences in these professional development workshops, their work toward earning college degrees and obtaining teaching licenses, as these experiences intertwined with their lives.

New Mexico is home to 22 Native American tribes, including 19 Pueblos. The Zuni Pueblo, located in western New Mexico and eastern Arizona, encompasses approximately 450,000 acres of land, where the Zuni have lived for thousands of years. The Zuni Pueblo's current population is approximately 9,494, with a $35,752 median household income. In the Zuni Public School District, encompassing over 600 square miles, the largest racial/ethnic group in the area is American Indian (96%), followed by Hispanic (3.3%), and White (.39%) (Deloitte, 2016). The school district is comprised of approximately 1,300 students and 77 teachers (National Center for Educational Statistics, 2016). Zuni is approximately 160 miles from the University of New Mexico's main campus, a three-hour drive on highway and two-lane roads, and a 45-minute drive to UNM's branch campus in Gallup.

We are anxious for you to meet our authors—our friends—who are Zuni tribal members, non-tribal members, current and former college students, college degree holders, staff members, community members, and PK-12 teachers. Throughout this book you will read about the authors' experiences as participants in ZETAC—their journeys to becoming teachers, and their challenges along the way. Each author writes a rich narrative of life experiences that helps the reader to understand the lives of Native Americans in 21st-century America. These authors are working to navigate two worlds— the Western world, that governs the laws of teacher licensure and the expectations of public schools; and the Native world, that strives to preserve and promote Zuni history, language, and culture.

Throughout this book, the authors discuss their roles in ZETAC, the benefits they received, the information they learned, and the support provided to them. In addition, they tell their personal narratives about their journeys in education. In the first section of the book, "Hearing Our Voices," the authors tell their life stories and their commitment to education in Zuni. Stacy Panteah explains her role in assisting in the administration of ZETAC and her role of support for all the participants. She also compares the educational world of decades ago with the opportunities available to students today. Shalay Bowannie describes her challenges as a young mother taking classes to complete her teaching degree. Kyle Martinez details his path to becoming a teacher and the struggles and successes he experienced along the way. Valarie and Sherry Bellson are sisters who tell their stories of being raised as foster children outside of Zuni, and what their lives have been like as adults returning to Zuni and serving their community.

The second section, "Working With and Within," highlights the work of teachers who integrate Zuni history, language, and culture in their classrooms through Project-Based Learning (PBL). Norene Lonasee explains how she teaches her preschool children Zuni history, language, and culture through her Heirloom Seed Project. Ray Hartwig and Joy Cushman are non-Native; they describe their experiences of seeking their own acceptance within the Zuni community. As high school teachers, they share their strategies for integrating PBL, Zuni culture, and public school district curriculum standards.

The authors hope you, the reader, will gain many insights from reading this book. Several authors articulated their hopes with these words:

> I hope readers will learn how innovative Zuni can be and that Zuni can move forward and adapt to things that are being presented.
>
> —Stacy Panteah

> My chapter champions volunteerism for all of humanity. When you invest in yourself, you are investing in the future of your family and community.
>
> —Valarie Bellson

> I hope readers will feel confident enough to try new things and just see what happens.
>
> —Ray Hartwig

> I want people to know they are not alone. Some can relate to at least one of our stories, and I hope they feel inspired.
>
> —Shalay Bowannie

> I hope people learn from reading my chapter that it is never too late to go back to school and complete any goals they may have. Next I want people to realize that it was not easy, growing up was tough, becoming a father was challenging, and completing school was tiresome, but it was all worth it!
>
> —Kyle Martinez

> I hope readers identify with choosing to be an urban Indian to learn and go back home to create different moments that move time forward into modernity.
>
> —Sherry Bellson

> I hope the readers find our Zuni beliefs, culture, and traditions interesting. I also hope the readers have a better understanding of our Zuni world.
>
> —Norene Lonasee

As you read these chapters, we hope that your understanding of the richness of Indigenous communities and the educational challenges faced by teachers, students, parents, and community members is enhanced. We also hope you hear these resilient and committed voices and that these voices inspire you to take action within your own professional practice.

References

Deloitte Data USA. (2016). *Zuni Pueblo, New Mexico*. [Data file]. Retrieved from http://datausa.io

National Center for Educational Statistics. (2016). *Zuni Public Schools*. Retrieved from www.nces.ed.gov

Acknowledgments

We appreciatively acknowledge the efforts and support of so many, without whom Zuni: Engaging Teachers and Community (ZETAC) and this book would not have been possible.

Thank you to Mr. Hayes Lewis, the executive director of the A:shiwi College and Career Readiness Center and former Zuni Public School District superintendent, who took a big leap of faith to work with two non-Native women from the university to implement ZETAC in the Zuni Pueblo. Mr. Lewis was our solid foundation, who kept the focus of supporting Zuni students and teachers at the forefront throughout this work.

Thank you to the W. K. Kellogg Foundation, who generously funded ZETAC and believed in us and our mission. Our program officers, Arelis Dias and Alvin Warren, supported and encouraged us as we implemented a new type of university-pueblo partnership.

Thank you to Kathy Meyer and Ellen Erlanger, Partnerships Make a Difference, for bringing their care and their expertise in service-learning and Project-Based Learning to Zuni, and for their continued support throughout the life of this project.

Thank you to former University of New Mexico President Robert Frank and Provost Chaouki Abdallah, for introducing us to this project beginning in the Office of the President, and for their understanding and appreciation of the importance of this university-pueblo partnership.

Thank you to Stacy Panteah, the administrative services manager at the A:shiwi College and Career Readiness Center, who held all the moving pieces together, including requesting scholarships, planning institutes, and mentoring and encouraging students. She also kept us laughing and well-fed.

Thank you to our Zuni Advisory Council: Dr. Carlotta "Penny" Bird, Dr. Breda Bova, Dr. Gregory Cajete, Dr. Theodore Jojola, Sarah Kostolecky, Hayes Lewis, and Stacy Panteah, for their expertise and guidance throughout this project.

Thank you to Amy Hathaway, the administrative assistant for the Department of Teacher Education, Educational Leadership, and Policy (TEELP) at the University of New Mexico. She patiently and expertly assisted us with all the financial transactions such a project requires.

Finally, thank you to the Krebs and Torrez families, (Paul and Jacob Krebs and Taylor, Kaleb, and Caroline Potter and Paul Torrez) for their encouragement of our dozens of trips to Zuni over the past five years, for their own interest and support of ZETAC and its success.

Contributors

Sherry Bellson, Zuni Tribal member, Zuni community member

Valarie Bellson, Zuni Tribal member, Zuni community member

Shalay Bowannie, Zuni Tribal member, university student

Joy Cushman, Zuni High School English educator, graduate student

Ray Hartwig, Zuni High School science educator, graduate student

Hayes A. Lewis, Zuni Tribal member, Executive Director, A:shiwi College and Career Readiness Center, Former Superintendent, Zuni Public Schools

Norene Lonasee, Zuni Tribal member, Zuni Head Start teacher, university student

Kyle V. Martinez, Navajo Tribal member, university student, novice teacher

Stacy Panteah, Zuni Tribal member, Administrative Services Manager, A:shiwi College and Career Readiness Center

Zuni Mural Designed by Zuni Artisan Edward Lewis

Zuni Mural Project

Hayes A. Lewis

The mural, designed by Zuni artisan Edward Lewis, is a unique visual addition to the A:shiwi College and Career Readiness Center located in the Pueblo of Zuni.

The mural is the first of many we hope to see on the exterior and interior walls of this higher learning center. The tribe is engaged in the process of establishing a Pueblo tribal college and has begun the transformation of the higher learning model from a Westernized conceptual framework to one that is also supportive of Indigenous people and communities. An important aspect of this process of change is to also change the physical environment to reflect ancestral knowledge and values and depict cultural images reflective of the tribe's development.

The mural is 11 feet in diameter and features a representation of a spiritual being on the left and a Zuni woman on the right. The spiritual being is depicted in the clothing of a rain priest and is playing a flute created from a reed and gourd. He represents the male and is caring for the corm plant, which has been with the people since emergence and represents the most sacred of plants in the Indigenous world. The song he plays entices the seeds to grow, brings the cloud people with rain (water), and allows life to flourish. The female represents strength and our Earth Mother with all her beauty and bounty, and a reminder that women are sacred beings that produce and nurture life in all forms and must be protected.

In the foreground is a bowl of cornmeal spiritually prepared for use with daily prayers of the people and offerings to ancestors. Inside the bowl are six ears of corn, each color representing one of the directions as well as the six Kiva societies of the people. They also represent all seeds that must be protected for future generations. The letter A, numeral 5, ruler, the small book depicting Ant people, and the pencil remind us of the changing world and environment in which we live. In spite of changes, we must hold on to scared knowledge and ancestral teaching and practices to sustain ourselves and the world. The education we provide must include cultural knowledge and skills, as well as the knowledge and competencies to succeed in contemporary society.

Rising over Do:wa Yalan:ne (Corn Mountain) is our Sun Father with rays of light energy, which also represent the six directions and are colored as since time immemorial: White-East, Yellow-North, Blue-West, Red-South, Multicolor-Upper, and Black-lower. Within the rays of light are depictions of our ancestors, our creativity, relations, places our people have traveled, and how they settled at the sacred middle place of the world: Ha'lona:wa Idewan:na (Shiwi:na-Zuni).

Part 1
Hearing Our Voices

1 Supporting Successes of Students and Community Members

Stacy Panteah

Close your eyes and imagine yourself living in the early years of the 20th century on the Zuni Reservation, when there were no schools or teachers around and formal education was not part of everyday living. Zuni Pueblo, located in the beautiful mountains near the New Mexico state line and approximately 14 miles from the Arizona state line, lies a Native American community with strong cultural beliefs where the use of the Zuni language for formal teaching is done by carrying on the traditions through oral teaching without outside resources. Only the surroundings are used as a *school* or facility to teach. The basic skills of learning how to measure were used with hands or some type of instrument. For example, Zuni women would make bread using one of their hands as a measuring cup to determine how much flour was needed. There were no cookbooks to read or measuring cups to use.

Now imagine yourself in the 21st century, where education is a requirement and students and community members are being provided an opportunity to participate; where all forms of formal education are being offered. Education in our Zuni community has become an important aspect of our students' daily lives, whether they are attending a pre-school class or are working on a doctoral degree with one of the universities. As Zuni tribal members, we are very fortunate to have a right to education that has been recognized by our tribal government.

Our elders before us didn't have the educational opportunities that are offered in today's world. I recall my grandfather telling me that he had to go to a boarding school when he was young, which was off the reservation. As the years went by, a Catholic school was introduced to the community, as well as a day school, and eventually the Zuni High School was opened. Although technology started evolving, it was not part of the schools in our community. So students did not have access to higher education at a community college, nor was technology available to them to take online courses.

Today, we have our own Zuni Public School District, which includes a high school, a middle school, and an elementary school. There are approximately 1,200 students attending those schools. Technology is available and used at each school site every day. In addition, our community now has a community college on the reservation. Courses from the University of New Mexico are offered at the campus. In comparison to what was available to my grandparents, my parents, and other elders as far as the educational opportunities, we are very fortunate to have it available now.

As one of the key support persons for Zuni: Engaging Teachers and Community (ZETAC) since the initial conception of this project, it definitely has been the most rewarding experience working with students, teachers, and community members. The initial goals of the project were to enhance the educational attainment of children in the Zuni Public School District by focusing on the continuing education, professional development and recruitment of teachers in Zuni. The services that ZETAC used to implement these goals have been unique because the core of the project involves learning about the Zuni culture and supporting Indigenous higher education in a rural community.

The tribe realized the need to establish its own school district, but there was still a need to hire certified teachers for those positions. Individuals who were non-Zuni, but certified, were usually hired to fill those positions. ZETAC has helped fill the need for Zuni educators in Zuni.

Since this was a new grant that was awarded to the Zuni Public School District and the University of New Mexico, the implementation had to start from scratch. By this, I mean that we had to create all the forms, brochures, flyers, etc., we needed for recruitment and documentation of a participant's involvement. With input from Mr. Lewis, former superintendent of the Zuni Public School District and Dr. Krebs, with the University of New Mexico, I created a majority of the documents to be used for the program, including the scholarship guidelines. In addition to the documentation, we established partnerships with various tribal programs and food vendors to assist the project during our professional development training.

Of course, as expected during most events held in our community, there was always food involved. During our professional development trainings and institutes, we were always prepared to serve refreshments and lunch to our participants. This would have not happened without the dedication and commitment of our administrative assistants, Ms. E and M. Q. Their professionalism in providing the support needed as well taking care of all the logistics during the trainings is to be commended.

In the initial starting of the project, we had 70 individuals who were college students, teachers, and community members who participated in the professional development trainings we offered, as well those who were enrolled as students with the University of New Mexico at the Zuni Campus. Over the course of the years, the need to retain teachers in the Zuni Public School District was becoming harder, as most out-of-state and non-Zuni teachers would stay a couple of years and then leave. The inconsistency of teachers staying in the district and leaving after being here only a couple of years was not a very positive thing for our students. To try to retain more teachers to stay with the Zuni Public School District, a grant was written by Mr. Lewis in collaboration with Dr. Krebs from the University of New Mexico to try and address how to sustain teachers in the community, especially our own Zuni individuals.

ZETAC offered professional development workshops for teachers on a number of various areas from classroom management to Zuni cultural activities to project-based learning. The majority of educational assistants in the district are Zuni tribal members. We encouraged them to enroll in educational degree programs so that each of them could earn a bachelor's degree and move up to become a certified teacher. This included assisting them with scholarship funds and books and providing them the support needed, since a majority of these individuals were non-traditional students. By providing these educational assistants with this support, they were able to empower themselves to be successful candidates for an educational degree program.

Although the services and support were available, we had some problems recruiting Zuni tribal members who were educational assistants to commit to becoming students to earn degrees to become teachers. There were several issues that we faced when trying to recruit Zuni educational assistants to become teachers. They were afraid to start the application process since they were non-traditional students. They didn't believe they had support at the administrative level at their school sites to provide them the time needed to attend classes. They did not want to become teachers because they were comfortable where they were as educational assistants. Also, many were afraid of change.

However, as time passed and the program was introduced into the community, more individuals became participants of ZETAC, and they enrolled in associate's or bachelor's degree programs with the University of New Mexico. There are a couple of participants who earned their Associate's Degrees in Early Childhood and have moved on to completing their Bachelor's Degree programs. There are also a couple of participants who have earned their Bachelor's Degree and have successfully gained employment as teachers with the Zuni Public School District. Two individuals successfully completed the Master's program with the support of ZETAC.

Currently, there are two individuals who are also in the process of obtaining their doctoral degrees. These are Zuni tribal members and are employees of the Zuni Public School District.

Although we had a steady number of students enrolling in educational degree programs, the administrative support from the school district slowly faded. With the change in administration in 2016, the support to complete the student teaching internship requirement was diminishing and served to discourage those who were trying to complete that portion of their programs.

Having to work closely with students and being able to monitor their grades gave me the opportunity to help the students with issues that arose. For example, as part of the ZETAC scholarship guidelines, students were required to submit their midterm grades. This requirement is in place so that if a student was failing a certain class, I was able to intervene and redirect them to a tutor or other resources they needed to improve their grades. This allowed them to maintain their GPA when final grades came out. Often students whose grades did not meet the criteria of the scholarship award were afraid to report their grades for fear of being dropped from the project. However, when we explained and provided them the support they needed, they understood the importance of meeting the scholarship guidelines thus encouraged them to accept the support being offered to improve their grades.

Another integral part of the project was the professional development training that was offered to teachers, educational assistants, and community members. The workshops covered a wide variety of topics but always included information about Zuni culture and traditions. Project-Based Learning training was and still is a major topic for those who have attended the sessions planned during the spring and summer sessions. A prime example of a successful project-based learning topic is a geology class that is taught at Zuni High School. The teacher incorporated the teaching of fetish carving as an opportunity for sustainable self-employment for his high school students. They learned this skill while learning about the different types of rocks. He requested assistance from a community member to teach the students how to carve the unique formations of a rock with the outcome of many beautiful fetish carvings.

One area of professional development that was always offered for non-natives was teaching of the Zuni culture. In our community, we expect non-native teachers to be culturally sensitive and know what the expectations are when living in our community. There are some non-native teachers who come to our community not knowing or understanding our culture or beliefs, therefore leaving them frustrated and having them leave with the misconception that Zuni is not a friendly place to live. Therefore, by having expectations of these teachers to know about our culture, the best way to share information with them was through some of the professional development training we had.

A prime example of sharing this information with them was the A:shiwi Core Values. These core values are taught in the home, in the community, and in the schools. We believe and follow these A:shiwi Core Values that are taught and carried on from one generation to the next. The A:shiwi believe that:

(1) **Hon ansammo le'na a:dek'yanna.**
We will live accordingly.

(2) **Hon i:yayyulashshik'yana:wa.**
We will respect one another.

(3) **Hon ko'hol lewuna:wediyahnan, wan hon i:tse'manna.**
We will think before we act and consider the consequences.

(4) **Hon i:yansatduna:wa.**
We will help one another.

(5) **Hon i:yanbeye:na:wa.**
We will give advice and counsel one another.

(6) **Hon i:yayyumola a:dek'yanna.**
We will be honest and trust one another.

(7) **Hon i:wichemana:wa.**
We will love one another.

(8) **Hon dewulashshi' iwillaba' a:dek'yanna.**
We will be kind and generous to one another.

(9) **Hon i:yanhadiya:na:wa, hon i:yayyu'hadiyahk'yana:wa.**
We will listen and pay attention to one another.

(10) **Hon delanko'ha:willi:wa.**
Be empathetic to one another.

(11) **Ihadiya:wa.**
Listen.

(12) **Don dehwan illaba.**
It is your turn.

(13) **Hom dehwan ukna:we.**
It is my turn.

These core values are important to carry on and we as Zuni people will not be able to sustain our culture without them.

Being a part of a project such as this has been quite rewarding, although there may have been a few challenges. Technology today has had a major impact on how education is now being taught in our community as well as how it is being utilized by our ZETAC participants to earn their degree.

Based on all the activities that we have had with this grant and the ZETAC program, I've come to realize that education is vital for survival in any community, whether it is on a Native American reservation or in an urban area. I feel that in today's society, one cannot set any high standards for a career unless one has completed a degree program. I myself have an Associate's Degree in Accounting, but I am not able to be a certified public account until I complete a bachelor's program. So that limits my opportunities for any chance of becoming a CPA.

We have several students who are pursuing their educational degrees. Without a teacher, they cannot meet the standards set by the state of New Mexico and our Zuni Public School District to become a teacher. One student in particular who has been on the program from the start has just graduated and earned his bachelor's degree to become a teacher. He is Native American and lives in the community. We need more individuals who are Zuni who live in the community to become certified teachers. This will give our children the sustainability they need for a continuous education from the same teachers because the current trend right now is that non-native teachers are being hired and only stay for a couple of years and then leave. This isn't good for our children. Continuity of teaching needs to be by the same individuals who will stay in the community.

Education in the 21st century in comparison to the early 20th century in our Zuni community has changed tremendously. With the increase use of technology and other available resources, anyone in our community can be empowered to become a successful individual by earning that degree to become a teacher or work in another professional field. With the support from the University of New Mexico, the W.K. Kellogg Foundation, and the Zuni community, it is an honor to work with this project and see the positive results that have impacted our community and the teaching of our students.

2 Is Teaching PK-3 a Good Fit for Me? Challenges Abound

Shalay Bowannie

I am the third child out of four. I have one brother, an older sister, and a little sister. I live in Zuni, New Mexico, and I have lived here all my life, apart from the six years I lived in Albuquerque. I grew up with a large family, with both immediate and extended members. There was no such thing as second or third cousins, great-aunts or great-uncles, or grandma's sister or brother. We are a cousin, auntie, uncle, grandma, or grandpa, simple and straight to the point. From time to time, we would go over to my *wowo's* (parental grandmother's) house and play there with our younger cousins or go to my auntie's house to play with our other cousin there. At family gatherings, especially as I got older, I felt out of place. While the majority of my family spoke Zuni, I didn't. I felt a bit embarrassed for not knowing or understanding very little at the time. Out of the four of us, my *baba* (older brother) spoke the language fluently, while my sisters and I could only understand bits and pieces of our sacred words spoken from the tongues of our elders. I did not realize how important and what big of a role the Zuni language played in our survival because our language is the backbone of our people and thus vital to our existence.

Being involved in my Zuni religion is important to me. My dad grew up traditional Zuni, knowing and participating in the religious part of it. He joined the military after high school, and when he came back, his beliefs in Zuni were gone. My dad's views of the religion changed, and no longer did he participate in any sacred ceremonies. My family has blamed the military for the reason why my dad is the way he is. My mom, on the other hand, was brought up Catholic and Zuni, but mostly Catholic. She would tell us stories of her and her siblings being woken up to go to church and having to wait after church for their parents, because they were busy mingling. As my siblings and I were growing up, neither religion was pushed upon us. Instead we were given the choice of what religion we wanted to believe in. It was nice to know that we had a choice, but I felt that I didn't need to choose because the Zuni religion is what we were surrounded by, thus making it a vital part of my life and something I was simply comfortable practicing.

I really enjoyed my elementary years, partly because the teachers made learning fun! I can't remember doing work or taking tests while in school. I remember doing centers, reading in groups, singing songs at circle time, playing outside, and overall just being a kid. I did have a difficult time because I was shy and quiet, and kids took advantage of it. My older siblings were more outspoken, social, and were in sports. I, on the other hand, remained shy and quiet, all the way into my high school years. I never liked going to school after elementary and couldn't wait until I finished high school. I was ready for a fresh start and ready to go off to school, where no one knew me.

After graduating high school, I moved to Albuquerque to go to school with my older sister for the fall semester. I attended the Southwest Indian Polytechnic Institute (SIPI), originally majoring in Culinary Arts and Hospitality Services Management. At SIPI, I enjoyed the small classes, the one-on-one instruction, and the small campus. It was there where I learned to come out and not be so afraid to speak out; it helped to have my sister and cousin there to help. Although many people might say that SIPI is not one of the best community colleges, I was always told, "It's what you make of it." I got my Associate's Degree in 2008, and then I only had two weeks to prepare myself as I made the switch from a community college to a university.

My first semester at the University of New Mexico (UNM) was surreal, partly because I never thought I would get that far in my education other than graduating from high school. I was excited but a little overwhelmed. I had to make the adjustment to having more than 400 students in each of my classes. Thankfully once I got into my degree program, the number went down to 30. I quickly learned if I wanted to succeed in my classes I must, of course, attend all required meeting times and make sure I introduced myself to the professors so at least they knew my name and I was not just another number. I made friends with fellow classmates, and they came in handy when notes were needed if I missed class. Last, I tried not to be afraid or embarrassed to ask questions because most likely I was not the only one who did not understand the information being taught.

At UNM, I changed my major to Dietetics. I wanted to major in something that would be of use when I returned home to Zuni. I decided not to stay on campus, but instead my cousin and I got an apartment. We commuted back and forth, and I was fine with that. I also decided to get a job. I had never had to get one thanks to my parents' financial support, but I decided it was time to start becoming independent. I applied at the UNM Children's Campus and got the position as a student staff employee. Thankfully they worked around students' schedules, so it worked well for me. It was there that I realized my enjoyment of working with and around little ones. I found myself enjoying going to work each day and dreading going to class. I had learned so much and had so much fun working there that I decided to apply for a permanent staff position and got it!

I was taking classes, but I began to get tired of going to school. Also, I was not doing so well. At SIPI, I was always on top of my academics; I was on the dean's list and maintained over a 3.5 GPA. At UNM, it was a different story. I was shocked when I received my first F in a class! I was too embarrassed to tell my parents. I was put on academic probation for the semester. I told my parents I wanted to take a break for a semester or two and just work because I was exhausted from taking classes. I did try to go back but withdrew from my classes and stuck with working, which I was content with.

In 2010, I found out I was pregnant! I took time off from work once our daughter was born and returned to work a month later. My boyfriend and I debated whether to remain living in Albuquerque or to return home to Zuni. We finally decided, with the cost of living expenses on top of daycare expenses, to move back to Zuni. I stayed home taking care of our daughter while my boyfriend worked. It was nice to take a break, but I wanted to do something more with my life. Don't get me wrong, I love my daughter, but I wanted her to be well taken care of. I, too, wanted to provide for her. In 2012, I enrolled at the UNM-Gallup branch, where I majored in early childhood multicultural education (ECME). It was extremely difficult to find the balance of being a new mom, taking classes, and trying to find time to study. I am forever grateful to have my family, my boyfriend, and his family for support. I didn't want to disappoint them this time around, so I worked my butt off and made sure I passed every single class, including math and science (as those two subjects are my weakest). In 2014, I graduated with my Associate's Degree in Early Childhood Multicultural Education.

This time I was not going to let this degree go to waste; I was going to put it into use. Zuni did not have any openings for educational assistants, so I looked for a job in Gallup. The Gallup Head Start was hiring, and I was asked if I also be interested in applying for the teacher position as well since I had my Associate's Degree. I was a little intimated, because I had never had my own classroom before, and I felt I was not ready to lead a class yet. I also applied at the Gallup McKinley County Schools, and to my surprise, I got a call from one of the elementary schools, and I accepted an interview. I am not very confident in interviews. I become nervous and my sentences don't come out right, especially when I am put on the spot. The day of the interview I practiced on my way to Gallup, so I wouldn't look too unprepared. I went into the interview feeling good, and once the interview was finished, I was so relieved. I went home feeling a bit anxious. With four in total being interviewed, I felt my chances of getting hired were very slim. I continued to look for other job openings, so I would not feel bad about not getting the position. I got a call the next day from the principal with a job offer that I quickly accepted. I have been working as a Pre-K assistant for three years now and loving it!

In 2016, I had my son, and I must say boys are a lot different than girls! They both are an adventure and are my life. I am still working toward my Bachelor's Degree in Early Childhood Education, but I am working at my own pace. Thankfully I have an advisor who understands that. The past couple of years have been difficult. During the year that I was pregnant with our son, my boyfriend had his religious obligation. With everything that was happening that year, on top of taking classes, the monthly obligations, being pregnant, and working, I found myself taking naps instead of doing homework or studying. After giving birth to our son in September, I realized I could not balance everything out. I could only handle so much, and I had reached my limit. I withdrew from all my classes that fall semester without regret. It was nice not having to worry about readings, quizzes, exams, or occasionally unintentionally missing class. Having that small break was worth it.

I finally registered for classes for the 2017 fall semester and was ready. As the semester started rolling, I had a death in the family. I don't blame nor do I use that as an excuse for my reason why I just let the semester slip out of my hands. It came as a shock; I didn't realize we would be losing part of the glue that held our family together. My focus on school was not there anymore; my family needed me, and I needed my family.

This new year came rolling in, and I knew it would be different and I had debated, once again, whether I should take a class or two. I finally settled on taking one class for now because I felt that it was all I could handle. I was so thankful I finished off the fall semester and passed my class; I could have done better, but that is okay. I sometimes feel the need to stop taking classes and be done with school completely because it does become too much to handle and worry about. But I am so close to graduating and getting my Bachelor's Degree. My kids are now my motivation to finishing. When I graduate, I want to come back to Zuni and work. It would be a nice change to help teach our Zuni children (and to be closer to home).

As I was working so hard to finish my degree, I had an opportunity for some support for my education. My second year into taking classes, in 2013, Mr. Lewis, our school district superintendent, shined a light on the need for more Zuni educators. Mr. Lewis, with the help of others, created ZETAC (Zuni: Engaging Teachers and Community) to encourage more Zuni educators in the public schools. My mom informed me about the program and told my little sister and me that we should apply. I was curious. I went to the first meeting during the summer of 2013. It was interesting and a great learning experience. There were not just Zuni educators there, but also other non-Zuni educators had joined in, as well community members. That week, we had been introduced to Project-Based Learning (PBL). Our presenters showed us ways of incorporating PBL into our classrooms. We shared our ideas of what we could not only do in a classroom, but also in the community. As the week went on, educators shared their experiences and ideas, and this made me more eager to be in a classroom! After the week-long workshop, I decided that being an educator is what I want to do.

What I enjoy about ZETAC is the fact that we have become our own little community. We learn from one another. I was glad that the program included students. It gave the adults time to collaborate with each other by sharing ideas or stories. During the last day of the summer workshop, we were wrapping up, sharing what we had learned that week. One student spoke out about her week, and she went into a deep conversation and expressed concerns about the Zuni language and how younger generations get frowned upon and unfortunately, made fun of.

I found that interesting, because as I was growing up, I never spoke Zuni other than the "slang" that many of the younger kids knew. I was afraid to even try because of my mom's story. She would tell us about how she and her sister were put on the spot by an elder because of the way they spoke Zuni. I could relate to the student who told stories of trying to speak the language. Like her, instead of being corrected, many of us were made fun of. That student was not the only one who expressed the embarrassment they felt trying to speak the Zuni language. Many students told their stories. A couple of the adults told similar stories, which surprised some of the students, not knowing that some of the adults had also been embarrassed too, while trying to speak the language when they were younger.

That day I walked out of the classroom thinking about what was said. I felt for those students and thought of what they felt especially to be embarrassed in front of people. I thought back to when I was in grade school and I would be called upon in math. Math is one of my weakest subjects, so when I was called on to answer a question, I was afraid and would keep quiet. This situation stood out to me, not only because the student who shared her story was unable to speak the language, although I could relate to her situation. But more importantly it stood out to me as an educator. To embarrass a child in front of a classroom, for me, is degrading as an educator, and something that should not be done. I thought about how we learn from one another, and her situation made me think of the type of teacher I wanted to be and the type of teacher I do not want to become. As an educator, I am there to teach children, not to shame them for what has not been taught to them. When I think of the educator I want to become, I think of those who have taught me. I am so grateful for their positive guidance, advocating, and teachings.

ZETAC has continuously and generously offered support and encouragement to those who want to further their education. The program has provided workshops, scholarships, hands-on learning, reaching out to the community, Project-Based Learning, implementing Zuni culture into classrooms, guest speakers from the community, and countless more supports. ZETAC has also included both middle and high school students (as mentioned) into the program. ZETAC has allowed me to continue on with my path to my degree. It has given me the tools and confidence I need to further myself in the field of education. I and many others who have benefited from this program could say without hesitation that ZETAC gave me, as well as other participants, the boost I needed to succeed, and I am thankful that this program exists so students like me can have the doors of opportunity opened for them, just like they have opened for me.

3   A Tribal Male Educator
My Experiences

Kyle V. Martinez

There are a several factors that influenced my decision to become a teacher. Although the first few are quite simple, there are two primary factors. First and foremost was to establish financial stability to help support myself and my family year around. The second was to become a teacher where the need for educators in the community remains high. There was a third factor that could easily have been the primary factor because it was personal. It all stemmed from a personal situation I experienced with my middle son. When my child was in the second grade, he and his classmates were surprised by the abrupt departure of their teacher. The details were personal and I respected that. Therefore, the details were never revealed, but the sudden void was disastrous for the students. These events occurred over five years ago. After the winter break in January 2012 I was assigned to his class as a long-term substitute; this would be my first experience as a long-term substitute and my most memorable. From this point forward, I knew teaching was my destiny.

My other reasons for wanting to become a teacher have to do with my aspirations in life before becoming a teacher became a reality. I wanted to coach and to remain a *hotshot wildland firefighter*. I wanted to keep substituting, and I wanted to coach my own children and the children from the community. Being a coach would provide common ground where I could help children at all levels on and off the court or field. I grew up playing basketball with my father as he was a coach and educational assistant. But it was from my mother, who also played, that I learned about the game. Without her knowledge and support, I may have given up playing basketball. I am proud to admit my entire family played, so I came from a basketball-rich heritage. All I ever wanted to do was play basketball and possibly coach it someday.

The final factor was to continue working seasonally with the U.S. Forest Service as an elite firefighter known as a *hotshot*. Hotshots are seasonal employees that come from a variety of backgrounds. They are teachers, contractors, students, and ranchers during the winter and hotshots in the summer. Most are permanent employees in a highly competitive career field. If you were not permanent, you were a seasonal, but we all knew it was the adrenaline and cohesion that kept you coming back. Considering all the factors involved I asked myself, "How can I teach, be a coach, keep firefighting, and give back to the children in the community?" This was well thought out. What happened next would have a profound effect on my career and where I am today. Let me go back and tell you about where I came from.

The Beginning

I was raised by my mother from a young age in a single-parent household. Times were rough. I have numerous memories of struggling to eat, and not having food to eat at times. All we had was Bluebird Flour and potatoes during the roughest of times. My mother would make homemade tortillas that tasted bland due to not having all the necessary ingredients (baking powder, salt, and lard). She used the same flour to make gravy to smother over the sliced and fried potatoes. During these earlier years, my family was my mom, my older sister, myself, and our younger brother. At this time, I was 11 years old, my sister a year older at 12 years old, and our brother at 3 years old. My mother had just divorced my father, and things went from bad to worst instantly. My mother insists she threw him out. Whatever the reason may be, I was glad because my father was abusive. My father made no effort to a part of our lives immediately after leaving us. He has reasons, and I respect that. I am happy to report our relationship has thrived more recently, and I am thankful for that. Although there are no discussions about the past, I know he is aware of the mistakes he made. I can see it in his eyes and in some of the stories he has shared with me. I forgive him. This is my memory of growing up, constantly struggling, but my mother always found a way to get us through and provide meals and clothing, and she still had time to discipline us.

My earliest memory of being in a school setting was visiting my father at work when I was around 9 years old. He worked as an educational assistant for several years and also a coach. My memories include his friends from work. One couple owned horses and a huge house, and another helped him coach basketball. After my parents separated, I began to hear stories of how well my father got along with students, how he mentored and coached them in sports, and his personal success as a player. Stories like these inspired me to become teacher at an early age, but those dreams did not last long because I felt only teachers had nice things like horses and vehicles. For reassurance,

I took my mother's determination and hardworking mentality into becoming a teacher. My mother retired 4 years ago after almost 40 years of service to the federal government. She never missed a day of work and would often drive 40 miles one way through snowstorms to get to work. Call this insanity or dedication. Either way, she knows what hard work is and continues to remind us to be thankful for having a job. It was not until 30 years later with my mother and older sister's guidance that I would follow and fulfill the dream of teaching. It took a while, but my mother invited a new man into the house, and eventually we welcomed a new sister. The youngest, my little sister grew up so fast. I remember times when she would latch herself on to my leg in fear of me leaving her. She was also my inspiration, for she earned her Bachelor's degree and encouraged me to stay on task and not fall behind. This time in my life was joyful; my mother was happy, and my stepfather was a great man. He has since departed us to join his Creator in another world. I will always be grateful for his guidance and support.

My Roots

I was raised in a small community within a satellite section of the big Navajo Nation Reservation named after the Ramah Navajo Band of Navajos. Ramah is located in southwest New Mexico about 45 miles southeast of Gallup, New Mexico. The Ramah reservation is surrounded by state, park, and private lands. This region is rich in diversity, culture, and tradition. There are multiple Native American tribes in this area and Mormon settlers that are connected to the explorer John Smith that have settled in this area. What sets us apart from the main Navajo Reservation is we have control of our own funding; we operate independently within the judicial system and have our own fiscal control system. I am 15/16 according to my census number; I do not know how they determine this exact number. I am aware that a census number is issued to all documented Native Americans; this is a way to document what tribe you are affiliated with and the specific amount of blood of that tribe. All I know is my grandmother is a great descendent of the infamous Jesus Eriacho that conquered the Pueblo regions in the 1800s. I am also aware that my grandfather has Apache roots from the great Apache nation of southwestern New Mexico. This makes my mother of Navajo and Mexican/Apache descendant. My father is full-blooded Navajo from an area not too far from where I currently reside. There is an old Navajo saying, "You are who your mother is. If she is Navajo, you are full-blooded Navajo. There are no half this or half that."

This is the easy part of my family tree; the hard part is explaining the Navajo clan system. Each parent has two paternal clans, one from mother and one from father. Their clans are passed down to the children and so on.

To keep it simple this makes me Bitter water (mother), born for Red Running into the Water (father) clan.

An introduction in my Navajo written language would be as follows: Yá'átééh shik'éí dóó shidine'é. ("Hello my people, relatives, and the rest of you.") Shí éíya Kyle Martinez yinishyé. ("My name is Kyle Martinez.") *Tódích'ii'nii* nish[į, dóó *Táchii'nii* báshíshchiin. ("I am of the Bitter Water clan, born for the Red-Running-Into-Water clan.") *Chí'shii* dashícheí, dóó Hal[soo' Dine'é dashíná]í. ("The Apache are my maternal grandfather's clan and my paternal grandfather is of the Meadow People clan.")

Becoming a Teacher

In the beginning I had no plans to become a teacher. I was set on graduating high school, going off to college, and becoming a veterinarian. I graduated from the same town I went to grade school in, Ramah. As I mentioned, it is small, tight-knit Mormon community in west-central New Mexico. After graduating high school, I followed through with one of my goals—going to college. My mission was to get out of my mom's house, not out of fear or retaliation, but to finish school and provide for her. After all the years of struggle, domestic violence, and uncertainty, I wanted to complete school, get a job, and help my mother out. I wanted to thank her by having her not work anymore and not worry about us making it. We all made it, we all graduated, and we all went to college. This made my mother happy, and she is proud of us to this day. During my second semester of college, my life changed in an instant.

I had to make the most difficult phone call of my entire adult life to my mother. The purpose of this call was to inform her she was going to be a grandmother. Without much thought and carelessness, I was about to become a father at a young age. The phone call is still the toughest thing I have had to do. After all the "don't do this, don't do that," from my mother, I had let her down. I tried to re-focus and complete my first year of college, but the pressure was overbearing. I did not want to finish the semester at that college, and before long I withdrew. After this the only thing I could do was pack up and move. I would enroll in a college closer to where I would be able to support my child.

The next few years were fast-paced, full of ups and downs and the realization of being too young to raise a family finally set in. Regardless I was able to complete the transfer and accept what would be my first Associate of Science degree. During this time, I was introduced to the world of firefighting and fire science. I immediately changed my major from becoming a veterinarian to forest management. I was still trying to adjust to being a father, and as quick as we created a family, the faster we realized we were not ready financially, emotionally, and psychologically. It was a quick six years, and it was all over.

While completing my degree and changing my major, I fell in love with fire. Firefighting came to me unannounced; it fell into my lap, as the saying goes. While I was raising a family and earning an associate's degree, I had the opportunity to earn credits while working during the summer. A summer co-op program established for Navajo residents in my area. I took six credit hours during the summer. My tribe paid 75% of the wage and the employing agency paid the rest. The agencies that offered a joint agreement with my college for summer employment were the NPS (National Park Service) and the USFS (United States Forest Service).

I was not too enthused about the NPS as their jurisdiction covered a vast area of open area and highly populated public parks. I was more interested to the high elevations and forested areas of the forest service. I was selected to be a part of the Range crew that would improve watershed projects and protect federally allocated land. I was a part of a five-man crew of older men; we assembled, repaired, and extended fence lines as project. One day I was pulled off our daily assignment to attend firefighting training known as Basic Fire Fighting. After completing this training, I was certified to go on fire assignments. Still, being a firefighter (let alone a hotshot) was far from my mind.

Later that summer I was called to go on my first fire assignment, and thus the spark was lit. My firefighting history took many twists and turns after this, but I have no single regret as I enjoyed every bit of it. I was fortunate to have worked on several types of crews: a Type 6 Engine (firefighting apparatus), a six-person Initial Attack module, Type 2 hand crew, and Type 1 hotshot crew. These organizations or branches are part of a huge fire-fighting family with a structure system similar to the military. All my fire experience led up to what I considered my pinnacle of wildland firefighting—smokejumpers, considered the pinnacle of firefighting for most, but being a hotshot is what I wanted to be.

The challenges of being a hotshot were being away from home for long periods of time, being in constant proximity of those you learned to love (and hate), and being pushed to the ultimate limit of what you are made of. The payoff was the comradery, the scenery, and the glory, and of course the pay was exceptional. I have fought fire in every state west of the Mississippi expect for North Dakota, Kansas, and Nebraska. While traveling to fires as a hotshot and to one hurricane relief assignment (New Jersey), I have been to North Carolina, Tennessee, Alabama, Georgia, Florida, and West Virginia. My first large fire was the Cerro Grande fire in Los Alamos, New Mexico. That one assignment put firefighting into perspective; it was dangerous and unforgiving, and I loved it all!

My First Teaching Experience

The next big adventure was becoming a substitute with the local school district. I substituted in elementary school and middle school, and I was immediately drawn to the diverse environment. I did this as a coworker from the Range Crew suggested I try it during the off-season. I enjoyed the diversity and change in different perspectives I faced while substituting. In time, I had enough experience to comfortably lead students following the teacher's lesson plans.

I was satisfied. I was employed seasonally; I searched for employment during the winters picking up odd jobs such as a tire repair technician, warehouse helper, and substitute teacher. I remarried and moved to Zuni, New Mexico. This move would have the greatest outcome, which I never anticipated.

It had been 14 years since I graduated high school, 10 years since I received my associate's degree, and 7 years being a hotshot. All my time at the latter was seasonal, leaving the winters open to substitute.

Zuni Public School District

In 2009, I applied to the Zuni Public School District as a substitute teacher. It was the first time I had to have a background check and to register for licensure through the state to become *certified* substitute. The school district also required us to attend a mandatory eight-hour orientation and complete three days of observations at various school sites. After completion we were placed on the *list,* indicating our availability to substitute.

I was remarried and starting a new family in Zuni. It would be three years later until I would realize I had to become a real teacher. What led to this were two factors: my children and my age. Being a firefighter is arduous, both in hard work and being away from family. I was finally ready to move on and find a job closer to home. Being a substitute was a perfect start. By this time we had a son in second grade and a daughter in the first grade. There were multiple occasions when I would ask him, "Hey, son, do you have any homework?" He would always answer, "No." This became a pattern for at least two weeks, and his response never changed. I began to convince myself that at second grade children were too young to have homework anyway. I was substituting full-time; the need for substitutes was high, and I was constantly being scheduled to sub.

Finally, I found myself at my son's school site and decide to visit his classroom on my first break. I wanted to confirm with his teacher there really was no homework. To my disappointment, his teacher that he began the school year with was on sick leave and had been for over two weeks. Why did we not get a notification? To replace the teacher, the school assigned a few educational assistants to rotate with hopes of continuing instruction and keeping the peace in the classroom. Upon my research these very generous assistants were following instructional guidelines to the best of their ability but had difficulty managing classroom behavior. The students, including my son, had become comfortable with different assistants. They no longer followed any rules, and the classroom became unsafe.

This was it. How could I ensure that my son and his classmates had a teacher? I was eventually assigned as a long-term substitute for his class. From this point, I began searching for a way to go back to school. One educational assistant remained in the class, for which I was grateful. She was dialed in. What I mean by this is she lined me out with activities and lessons that helped me prepare daily. My main mission was to establish discipline. Up to this point the children "ran over" the educational assistants and harassed one another. After establishing rules, I was determined to guide them any way I knew how, with the help of my aide and the bilingual instructor.

The aides assigned to this class were extremely helpful. They both expressed their passion for working with children and had high hope for all the children. What impressed me the most was how they continued to help the students regardless of the challenges. I owe them a great deal. Part of the re-igniting the spark to earning a bachelor's degree stemmed from a particular staff member who always encouraged me to go back to school. I stayed with this class until the end; they all were promoted to the third grade. After getting down the routine, the children were amazing! They will all have a special place in my heart as being the "first" to finish the school year with me. Only one thing would make this experience better, which is being a certified teacher with a bachelor's degree. This opportunity would present itself a few years later after this part of my life.

Going Back to College

I went on to being recommended as a long-term substitute by the principal at the elementary school. I substituted in grades three, four, and five for the next two and half years. Then in 2013, while I was filling in as a long-term substitute, I was approached by my principal. She demanded me to visit some folks from The University of New Mexico (UNM) at the local UNM branch which, at the time, was located in Zuni. At this time the UNM-Zuni branch was offering entry-level courses and was a wonderful option for high school graduates from the local high school. I met with Cheryl and several other representatives from UNM sponsoring the ZETAC initiative. These members, from the school district, included Mr. Hayes Lewis and Stacy Panteah, and later Audrey Eustace. I felt confident my associate's degree would propel me within two years of completing a bachelor's degree. I was way off, due to the classes I took not being able to be applied to a teaching degree. Fifteen years had elapsed. The people from UNM told me it would take me four years at the earliest. The second obstacle was funding.

After consulting with UNM and viewing my projected scheduling I was at a loss for words. How could I do this? There was no way I can afford this, plus I was too old! I left that day feeling helpless. I knew deep down I wanted to pursue my goal of becoming a teacher, and so did my wife. I continued as a long-term substitute that year leading into the summer of 2013. It was at this time I received an email, a flyer advocating teacher and community involvement through a joint partnership of UNM and the W.K. Kellogg Foundation. The superintendent and UNM's College of Education were going to host a summer institute promoting cultural significance and awareness in the school district. They were recruiting through a venture project titled ZETAC: Zuni Engaging Teachers and Community. Along with Mr. Lewis and his associates I was able to get answers on enrollment. I owe a lot to these individuals and more.

I was intrigued. Was this the answer I had searched for? Did I even meet the criteria? Was there even a criterion? I had to ask. I inquired, and the response was, "Attend and you will find out." I signed up for this institute, the first of many to come. Unfortunately, the firefighting business took priority; I had a family. As a substitute, I was not eligible for summer pay, and I had to take this chance at making extra money to support my family. If I was only a permanent employee with the school district—another spark was lit.

Thanks to ZETAC

I remember driving to Colorado en route to a fire assignment and making the call to cancel my RSVP for the summer institute. The people in charge were not disappointed, they were supportive, and I still appreciate this act of kindness to this day. I missed the summer institute but soon found out they were going to host a fall institute. This was perfect! I would register and attend no matter what. Prior to attending I was approached by several staff members expressing their appreciation for substituting their students and keeping order in their classrooms. They were amazed at how the students responded to me. They also acknowledged a shortage in certified teachers, especially Native American male teachers. If I needed more assuring, this was it. I now had the support of my wife (which was and still is never ending), children, administration, and now the teachers. Within this time I had questioned what ZETAC was all about to several staff members and all their responses were positive. They told me ZETAC would pay for me to go back to school, as long as I could get good grades. I thought to myself, *I can do this. If I study hard, I can earn passing grades, and my wife is from here. We do not plan on leaving.* The plan of retiring in Zuni was in the discussion quite frequently, and I was fine with that.

I finally met the ZETAC coordinators and the UNM staff members that made it all possible in the fall of 2013. I also was enrolled as a full-time student, making fall 2013 my first semester under ZETAC. At first, I was eligible for assistance using Pell Grant by applying through FAFSA, the Free Application for Federal Student Aid. This lasted for two or three semesters. What ZETAC offered was scholarships to students under the program plus stipends for books and supplies at the UNM bookstore.

This contribution made it all possible for me to be where I am today. Following a series of project-based learning (PBL) institutes, I noticed a major increase in attendance at ZETAC events. The word had gotten around about PBL and ZETAC workshops, their hospitality, and their professional presenters. This was amazing. I was back in school, I was more disciplined and determined, and I made the honor roll my first semester. I continued to enroll into each semester, including summer semesters. I received my second associate's degree in 2015. This time it was an Associates of Arts degree. I was accepted into the undergraduate program soon after and on pace to graduate in the fall of 2017.

ZETAC has awarded me financial scholarships for maintaining a GPA of 2.0 or above since 2013. I held a GPA above 3.0 throughout my undergraduate program. I finished with a 3.5 career GPA. ZETAC allowed me to focus on my classes by supporting me with book purchases using the UNM bursar account. Without ZETAC I honestly do not believe I would have made it this far. There are many challenges being a full-time student while raising a family and working.

I applied to the Zuni Public School District (ZPSD) and was selected to a permanent educational assistant position in 2014. Entering the undergraduate program meant the beginning of the student teaching phase of the program, which requires three semesters (typically the last three) of student teaching, from 5 hours a day in the class to 7.5 hours a day in the final semester. I am fortunate to be identified as a paid long-term substitute regardless of my status I have my own class now. Determination and support through ZETAC made this all possible.

Student-Teaching

My experience as a student has been tremendous. I have the advantage of being able to compare what I have endured these past 4 years to how it was 20 years ago when I first entered college. I look at it as a blessing in disguise, having a family, and witnessing first-hand the shortage of teachers in the community has motivated me to complete my undergraduate studies. There were many challenges along the way, such as financial stability, family commitments, and prioritizing school work, but nothing was going to keep me from graduating. On December 16, 2017, I graduated from the UNM College of Education with honors, Cum Laude, with a Bachelor's in Elementary Education and a concentration in Social Studies. I have fulfilled my destiny of earning my degree and becoming a permanent employee with the school district as a teacher. Without ZETAC, ZPSD, and UNM this dream of becoming a teacher would not be possible.

Acknowledgment

I want to acknowledge and thank my wife, children, and family for supporting me through my studies. There were several family events we could not attend because I had homework to do. There were many occasions when family and friends visited and I was too busy to break away from my assignments long enough to converse. Thank you to my sisters for setting the bar high and leading by example. Thank you to my mother for everything you have done for me and my family. Without all your support, this would not have been possible.

A very special thanks goes to my wife for believing in me and always supporting me. She will forever hear me say, "It will be over soon. The payoff is what matters most." She was there through it all and managed to keep the household in order. We did this together, and I will forever be grateful for her patience and understanding.

My hope now is to inspire my own children and prove to them anything is possible. You are never too old to go back to school. This journey has been a life lesson in communication, discipline, and integrity. It has been a long journey, and my family has experienced it with me. In 10, 20, 30 years I want my children to be proud to tell their friends and their families, "My father is a teacher and a coach." I want them to remember me as a person who says "Hello" to everyone and takes time to chat with people. If I can make a person happy by greeting them, I will. Knowing that I have put a smile on a person's face, even for a second, means a lot to me. If I can do that, imagine the effect I can have on a student's life. Most of all, I have inspired my younger brother to go back to school to earn his degree, which he will receive in May 2018. Good job, brother, and thank you for your words of encouragement!

4 Finding My Voice as a Zuni Woman

Valarie Bellson

My Early Schooling

I started my school career in Zuni at Zuni Head Start and continued to attend the Zuni school system until the fourth grade. In fifth grade, I was in school in Utah as a part of the Church of Jesus Christ of Latter Day Saints (LDS) Indian Placement Program. My older sister, Michelle, was the first participant in our family, and I met her foster family when they came to visit our family on the *Rez* in Zuni. I guess I felt this was something I wanted to participate in as well. Now, as a 43-year-old woman, I do not even think I realized what kind of life-changing decision this was. I wonder now, what did my parents think about all this?

We got connected to the Mormons through my grandmother. She lived in the Middle Village, which is the original adobe structure that is in the center of our Pueblo. The Mormon settlers came and wanted to have church meetings in the Middle Village in Zuni, so she and my grandpa opened up their house to them. At some point we met Michelle's foster parents. After Michelle left, they would make it a point to come visit Zuni during some of their summer vacations. So they knew my family and background, and they saw how my parents grew up. My parents were very young parents, so there was always a connection with this foster family.

When I went into the placement program my first year, I was placed with a family in Kearns, Utah. I was in fifth grade. The second year I was given to a family in Riverton, Utah, which was a farming community. I believe I was ready to leave my Zuni community because people were mean-spirited to me and to my family name. I learned this was not my shame, but the shame of the adults who had gone before me. My last name is *Bellson*. My grandfather is Navajo, and he married my grandmother, who was Zuni. She already had three children, so she and her Zuni children took my Navajo grandfather's last name. That's why we didn't know we were bad people until we got to school. When I started kindergarten, I remember peeing on myself on the playground because Zuni kids would call me *hathiwkwi*, or witch, which is not a nice memory to remember. The meanness of the students and the lack of any adult stepping up to stop this name calling left a pretty big negative impression in my mind. My life took a major change, in many aspects, when I chose to continue my education in Utah and not Zuni.

My foster family in Utah lived outside of town, so I only got to see my sister, Michelle, on weekends. Michelle's foster family would usually pick me up on Friday, and after dinner on Sunday evenings the two of us would go to her bedroom and cry because we knew I would have to leave soon, and we would not see each other again for another week. I think a lot of the other Indian Placement Program students did not get financial support, or even a letter or a telephone call from their parents. But Michelle and I knew that every time Mom got paid from her job in Zuni, the following week we would always be waiting for something in the mail because she would send something—money, holiday things—and we knew we were not forgotten for the nine months that we left Zuni because she was very consistent, every year, having those little care packages for us.

I have wondered why my parents did not try to change our minds about becoming foster children in Utah because to participate in this program, we had to be baptized as members of the LDS Church. Even today, my dad, my sisters, and I are the only ones baptized as members of the church; my mom has never shown interest in becoming a member, and we have never asked her to join.

I was always moved around to different foster families, and in all of this, that's where as an adult I recognized that the *little girl* in me is important. I was never asked, "Do you want to go to a different foster family?" I was told. So when I would move and try to settle with a new family, the adults would tell me, "This is what is wrong with you. This is why you are here." So imagine hearing that all the time, like they don't want you there because you had more friends than the rest of the kids. I also remember music lessons were a reward for the kids in their family. They said, "Valarie is not going to music lessons. Just you guys." Well, I would have loved to have had music lessons. So that's where, at a young age, I learned not to ask, and I realized the little girl voice in my life wasn't important.

When I was introduced to the Zuni Core Values through ZETAC, I found a real passion that lies within the Core Values. I believe if we could instill these character traits within our little ones, they would be able to grow as fully formed persons with character, where as adults, they won't be the alcoholic, be the drug addict, be the abuser, because they are being heard right now, instead of when they are 30 or 40 years old.

I went to Utah—a completely new part of the country—knowing this was not the Rez. If I felt awkward and different in Zuni, these differences were magnified ten times more in my new environment. When I started school there in fifth grade, I became what was called the *token Indian*. I hated any history class where we discussed Indians at any level because after a concept was shared, I always asked something like, "Is that how things really are? Do you still live in a teepee?" How should I know, right? At such a young age, I already knew and felt whatever we were being taught in history or science was not accurate. As an adult I've come to the realization that the classes I choose to take now are basically classes reeducating myself in my Zuni-ness. I always felt I was lacking and flawed, not good enough to be a part of the Zuni life and community, as well as not good enough to fit into the white world.

To this day, my mom or dad never had any part in our homework or completing school projects, or parent-teacher conferences, so I think that is why I over-compensate with my two kids. I live with my parents now, and my mom says to me, "Why are you not helping them with their homework?" "Why are you not at the school helping out?" and I think to myself, *Well, you never did that for me*, but I don't let that out. I don't speak that to the world because I know my mom did what she could. She was a teenage mom, and she was the older sister of seven siblings, so she had a tough time. I never really asked her about her experience, but she would just say to me, "You will not be a teenage mom."

Going to College

I am fortunate to have become one of the first members of my family to obtain a college degree. I was prepared to handle college academically from the teachers of Hillcrest High School in Sandy, Utah. I made this choice because I knew I would be the only Zuni Indian on campus. I honestly believe that because I had no sense of self, in the sense that I did not believe I was a good enough person, I could represent the Zuni Tribe and represent my family in a positive manner. I got my college degree by myself, without a child or a boyfriend. I am truly unique in that I experienced college the way college should be experienced—sharing a dorm and apartment with a roommate, all of that.

But there's another important part of this story, about why I think I was able to succeed, and that's because I was protected. I love sharing this story. During my first year of college, my parents would drive me the nine-hour drive to Cedar City, to Southern Utah University, and then come pick me up for holidays and summer break. But once they gave me a car, I never felt like I was going by myself. I wasn't afraid. I always felt protected. I finally understood this when I received my Zuni Map Art Book, entitled *A:shiwi Awan Ulohnanne The Zuni Underworld* (Enote & McLerran, 2011), as a ZETAC participant. When I looked at those maps in the book, all the places I was driving through, I was with my people. I don't know how much more I can convey that it was truly sacred, and I didn't get it until 20 years after. I didn't know why I felt protected until I looked at the book from ZETAC and saw that that whole trip was through the area of the Zuni migration. My people were there!

Another time, during Native American Education Week, we invited the Zuni Olla Maidens to go. The Zuni Olla Maidens are a group of women who are famous for dancing with beautiful olla pottery on their heads. The pottery are coil pots that were once used to carry water to Zuni homes and families. The Zuni Olla Maidens are memorable because of the beautiful, colorful clothing they wear as well as the intricate handmade turquoise jewelry they wear.

The Olla Maidens needed a driver, so my dad volunteered to drive them. He told me they were driving west and that as soon as the ladies saw the San Francisco Mountain peaks, they started singing, and they sang all the way past Flagstaff and on to Cedar City.

He let them sing and finally asked, "Why are you singing?"

They answered, "Don't you know? We are singing to our people. They have been waiting for us. This is our first time to where you are taking us, so we are singing for them, and we are taking them with us."

When they arrived, the Paiute elders were there, and they said, "We have been waiting for you. Where have you been?"

I didn't love myself at this time. I didn't know what was going on, but all these elders seemed to be telling me that *is* why I chose this place to come to school. I had never thought of myself as a leader, but I ended up being the multicultural representative for the student body, and then a group of young women wanted to start a local sorority, and it's still there. In the end, I think Southern Utah gave me the tools to really be of service.

Even with all this going on, I believe I knew alcohol would play a negative role in my life, and that's part of the whole cloud of why I chose to leave my community and my family at such a young age. I was running away from the effects of alcoholism and the dysfunction we were all already living under. My father was an alcoholic before my sister Michelle was born. I think our mom made a choice to stop drinking because she knew our sense of family would be lost. Someone has to lead, right? So my father and memories of him are not great at this time because he chose not to be present in our lives 100%. He would leave our trailer home for months at a time without any contact. Then he would appear in our lives again, acting as if he hadn't been gone for months. Then he wanted to proceed living life with us. I knew it was our mom who was working two jobs to support three daughters. She worked as an educational assistant for 32 years with the Zuni Public School District, and she produced beautiful award-winning needlepoint jewelry at our home.

Even with all this, I still started drinking during my sophomore year of college, and I don't even know how I graduated. I started drinking because when I would come home from college, people my age were already married and had kids. They would say, "What are you doing? You're not with anybody?" My worth was being measured by whether I had a boyfriend, or if I had children. I think that's how I ended up majoring in sociology, because I was always thinking about the comments people made about me like, "Who are you?" I was always chasing my identity and worried if I fit in. At such a young age, I was being labeled, and this steered me into choosing sociology as my major. This way of thinking is what I connected with ZETAC. I connected with ZETAC. Thus, that is what I identified with and kept coming back to.

People would say to me, "You are going to be a great teacher," and so literally I thought, *I ought to be in the classroom.* But then with this alcoholism, if I didn't quit drinking, I would be just like everybody else—drink myself to death. It was that bad. My grandmother died from complications of alcoholism and diabetes, so I could have gone that route, but now that I think about it, I also kept hearing, "You're going to be a great teacher," but in my thoughts it was, *A teacher for the community . . . for the parents . . . for the community.* When I think about my grandmother, she did not see any of us do what we are doing because she died so young. For myself, I was going to be dead by 40. Now I'm 43, and at one of my conferences, a lady came up to me and said, "You are going to be the grandma for the Zuni people." I never thought of that, but those kinds of statements really build up against any kind of doubts I have. That's the stuff that keeps me going.

ZETAC has helped me become that *grandma to the Zuni People.* I became a participant of ZETAC in the spring of 2013. The experience was so amazing and empowering because I was attending classes that were being led by some amazing ladies from outside our community. I remember feeling so alive, thinking, *Where did these people come from?* I remember feeling so validated after 20 years of feeling like no one in my community understood me, or my want or desire to build Zuni up with positivity and empowerment. What got me so excited and inspired? Well, it was reading and being introduced to the *A:Shiwi Core Values.* This piece of literature was created by a group of Zuni educators from the Zuni Public School District, along with some Zuni community members.

I just remember feeling like the Core Values were going to be my guide in connecting with members in my community. This was my *ah ha* moment because I had struggled so much in my personal life and the little professional life I had created because I really didn't have a guide or direction on anything, period. But once I read those words, I knew I was a *Shiwi* woman who wanted and practiced respect, who practiced listening and sharing, who had empathy, who had love, who wanted to be heard, who wanted to be given a chance to live and practice these values on a daily basis.

With the *A:Shiwi Core Values* as an important tool in my life, I embraced the words of the Core Values and started believing and becoming an engaged and involved parent within the Zuni Public School District. All the amazing educational institutes I began attending through ZETAC gave me the confidence and the tools to truly believe my voice as a woman, a wife, a parent, a community member, and a leader who was worth listening to. I started attending PTO meetings to support the schools. In 2014, I got nominated by a group of teachers and was elected to become the treasurer of the PTO. In 2015, I got nominated and elected to be the president of the PTO. During this awesome year, the ladies I worked with helped create two very awesome traditions we are still practicing.

One of those traditions is the pizza coupon we distribute to celebrate 100 days of attending school. These coupons go to anyone in the entire school—the students, teachers, teaching assistants, support staff, and bus drivers and transportation department. Our local pizzeria, Chu Chu's, sponsors this giveaway. I am proud to have started this new tradition with our PTO parents because it is something our school community looks forward to each year. Another tradition is the making and distribution of homemade Valentine's Day cards for our young children, teachers, and support staff. These cards say, *Hon i:wichemana: wa*, which means "We will love one another"—one of our Zuni Core Values. As a PTO we wanted to set the tone in our school community using the words of our Core Values to validate the importance of each child and adult we come in contact with, making this positive change to acknowledge the individuality and uniqueness of each young boy and girl. Some of those who helped us make these cards were serving as parents to the little ones, even though they may have actually been their siblings because their parents have passed away. It is heartbreaking to me to learn about these situations, but it built up a passion in me to be that voice and that leader for parents and families in my community.

Though this all seems so cheery to have accomplished these things, the reality is it has been a battle with many hurdles and obstacles within the ZPSD educational system. The reality is, I have felt that although I have my higher education background, it is still not good enough and my voice and ideas aren't at that level of a teacher who is accredited and licensed. I have issues with being called out as a parent who complains when I am merely asking questions. I feel I have yet to be taken seriously, but this lack of being credible is driving my passion. The more I have been shut down, the more I will stand up for myself and for those parents who actively participate and are engaged in their children's education. Being an active participant in ZETAC has given me this foundation.

My husband, Rodney, and I are currently serving our second year as parent representatives of Zuni for the Johnson O'Malley Program and the Indian Education Committee for our school district. We have been fortunate to participate in various conferences through the state of New Mexico. In April 2016, I was blessed to be elected to be a national board member for the National Johnson O'Malley Association. I was honored with this title by being voted for by the state of New Mexico's Native parents who attended the national conference in Albuquerque. My role is to be the advocate for all Native children and parents in securing federal funds from Congress every year.

When this journey began for me, I never thought of myself as a leader in any capacity. I was into participating, but not leading. I believe I started truly seeing myself as a leader when a community member looked me in the eye and told me I started becoming a leader when I became a parent. I embrace this because it is true. We all become leaders when we become parents. Now I am taking it another step further when I know I am the voice of parents and children in my community. I am the voice who will champion for families. I am the voice who will question and advocate for higher quality and standards in education for the Zuni community. All my life I always questioned why I never fit in or why I was not like everyone else. Now I know I am the strong voice, giving support to anyone in my community who may feel the same way. *Ihadiya:wa*—listen. *Don dehwasn illaa*—It is your turn. *Hom dehwan ukna:we*—It is my turn (A:shiwi Core Values).

Reference

Enote, J., & McLerran, J. (2011). *A:shiwi Awan Ulohnanne: The Zuni underworld*. Zuni, NM: A:shiwi Awan Museum & Heritage Center.

5   Struggles and Perseverance within a Western System

Sherry Bellson

Keshi, my name is Sherry Bellson. I am a 41-year-old mother of three from the Pueblo of Zuni in New Mexico. As a teenager I chose to leave the reservation to pursue my education. Growing up in the reservation life, my parents let me leave home at the age 15, my freshman year of high school. For the most part, the choice to leave was based on my own negative personal choices. Overall, I was running away from the bad things I did. I realize now that all the disrespect that I had done to myself and others was so I could fit in with what I thought was cool at the time. When a brother from the church came to interview me, he was not sure he wanted to deal with me; I could see it on his face. I bore my soul to a man of God, and he accepted the responsibility of helping me want to improve on my life. It was upon stepping off the bus in Utah that I learned life was much tougher and harsher off the reservation, and trying to fit in was a spirit breaker.

Over the course of three years (ninth, eleventh, and twelfth grades), I lived with four different foster families and attended four different schools in the Salt Lake City and Provo suburbs. Being displaced, every step of this journey was about self-discovery and self-acceptance. It was extremely difficult to stay rooted in who I was and pursue who I was striving to become. The fusion of cultures, music, and the social buzz of society were static electricity, but Zuni customs and traditions kept me holistically grounded and aware of my social identity. When I felt lonely, sad, and beaten down, I made an offering and prayed for solace, strength, and courage from my ancestors. In the Zuni custom, my grandfather taught me to reach out to my ancestors when in need by making *a de:haken:na*, a food offering to leave with my prayer. I found myself reaching out for spiritually connections to other kids in my school—the Mexicans, Thai, Laos, Polynesians, and Asians—because they did the same ritual at their homes. They gave offerings, like me. What my foster families never understood was the colored folk treated me as an equal. We were all struggling to fit in. We were all fighting to survive a day in the skin our heavenly Father blessed us with. We were all displaced. As Generation X we were seeking our American Dream while encountering bullying, discrimination, and self-doubt. We encountered the concrete jungle together.

General academics and seminary were the main areas of study at my new high school. The standards were higher than on the reservation, and the curriculum was harder. I struggled with math. During my senior year, a Chinese immigrant helped me through with great patience. Art, creative writing, college prep English, and photography I & II were my favorite classes. Seminary aligned the religious community with core values and academics. Academics used the model of project-based learning, and seminary utilized the model of service-learning. Overall, seminary was a bonus to my life's education because it created a social conscience. It helped keep me grounded on what was right and wrong and what was fair and just as a human. I was homesick at times, and talking Zuni to my family over the phone helped calm my soul and helped me endure my choice. I mowed the lawn to pay my accumulated phone bill . . . aahh, the smell of fresh-ut grass.

In retrospect, this experience strengthened me for return back to the reservation at age 21 because I learned to adapt, be flexible, and appreciate my culture's teachings, and also because I was ready to give back. As an adult with a family, the realization that I have overcome so many struggles and adversities is remarkable. I have a purpose.

My sister's death was a significant event that changed our family and myself. After two or so years in limbo, the reality was my sister taught me to lead through engagement, service to self, community, and the world-at-large. After studying and learning to deal with my grief, my life slowly started shifting through positive social changes to myself and for my community and so I could fill my purpose in the world. I remembered reading *The Divine Comedy*, which was how I saw myself, going through the different levels of hell; my moment of enlightenment had Carlos Santana playing "Samba Pi Te" in the background. I had to struggle to appreciate life.

My late sister's teachings allowed me to dig deep, to look take a good look at myself. Project-based learning and service-learning have allowed me to move forward and contribute positively through civic engagement to my pueblo's struggles through all social stratifications we've met since being conquered.

The core values of *Hom dewulashi iwillaba ahdekyanna* (We will be kind and generous to one another), *Hom i:wichemanawa* (We will love one another. . . [We will love ourselves]), and *Ohm i:yayyulashik'yanna* (We will respect one another) helped me to become a community advocate, working to create positive social change for my community's prosperity and longevity through civic engagement and positive people connections.

My mission is to create opportunities for the youth of the community so they will know they are intangible assets because they are 21st-century learners capable of challenging their community's social stratifications. When this shift occurs, it will be because education was brought to the culture. We need to incorporate the students to be responsible stewards to their community. As a collective voice a tipping point will begin, creating a shift when we give moments to voice, hear, and learn about the flights of our own people.

How Great Leaders Inspire Everyone To Take Action, by Simon Sinek (2009) taught me that an aspiring leader vs. an inspiring leader is anyone who can talk the talk as well as walk the walk. As a people, we cannot move forward from our historical trauma until we map our community's heartbreak. We need to know about the policies that govern us on the reservation, in New Mexico, and in the United States. As tri-citizens we need to learn together to enforce positive changes for our future: the children.

As an inspiring leader, I want my community to know we can challenge the status quo of the community so we are no longer kept marginalized. Let's become experts by implementing the statistics and logistics of our community by taking a proactive stance for the future. I want to teach our community that we are an indestructible people who deserve to live a quality life.

Making critical connections about the policies governing the pueblo of Zuni has been a major connection of my purpose within the community. A history of elections for our community is a tool we can use to steer away from what hasn't worked and to look for new ways to walk peacefully in modernity. We are having trouble letting go of the past, so we haven't been able to catch up with the future.

As a Native woman, reaching out to professionals outside of the pueblo has been the connection that has been most resourceful and impactful for me. My mother, who was a teaching assistant for 32 years with Zuni School District, worked with teachers who nurtured our spirits through education. Ms. J taught me reading is important; if you don't know how, people will take advantage of you. Ms. E taught about etiquette and why manners are important; so you will treat people with respect, as well as being treated respectfully. They are a part of my life's foundation. A recent teacher of my daughter's taught me Native people need to learn about the policies that govern them to make community choices with positive impacts. Ms. M has taught me that lobbying is not only to influence people but also to reach out and help people make political choices for our community that benefit the greater good. Native communities across the nation continue to face the realities of drugs, alcohol abuse, violence against women, diabetes, loss of natural resources, and inequalities in education. As Natives our logistics surpass the national rates in all of these categories. So, how do we harness these social stratifications and take back control of our communities? We make connections with people who nurture the souls and hearts of the things we love and care about—our people and ourselves.

We make these changes by becoming engaged and educated about the issues that are most important to us as individuals. This beautiful pueblo with a rich history is dominated by bilateral oppression. We keep each other down. The negative attitudes at our schools impact our students emotionally, psychologically, spiritually, and physically. They need positive affirmations as well as emotional stimulation to become whole. Our students are being bullied by the systems placed over them.

As a parent, my concerns and advocacy for my three children have been met by educators who have literally stated that I have no credentials and how dare I question their pedagogy. As a community we need to support *Restorative Justice* and *Readiness To Intervention* processes in schools and classrooms because we are losing students due to lack of poor relationships in schools. The decline in graduation rates, the decline in enrollment, and the *F* grades our schools have received should be serious indicators of our instability to educate effectively. Because I don't hold steady work doesn't mean I'm not an affluent member of my community. Parents are our children's first teachers. Schools support the direction of the community in which they are serving. My wealth is in terms of family, education, and positive connections. *I love Zuni. I am home. That is my wealth.*

The learning opportunities presented by ZETAC have been invaluable. I have learned to turn negatives into positives by using my personal experiences to create positive professional opportunities. By building respectful communication and building trust, my sister and I have been able to give back to our community through volunteering. We are here to make a positive difference. We are here to help. We have skills and knowledge that ZETAC has honed. Through ZETAC, my full circle has allowed me to be innovative, exceptional, and extremely proud of being a Zuni woman. My new membership in organizations like Partnerships With Native America, Native American Voter's Alliance, Strong Families New Mexico, and ZETAC have given me opportunities to walk the walk and talk the talk. ZETAC's professional development workshops have been a blessing because they give me the platform to speak my mind, along with being able to be a guide on the side for others seeking positive energy.

Ultimately, my engagement and partnering with ZETAC has led me to the next phase of my community outreach. Currently I am canvassing our community to conduct a community assessment to create a community voice. Education is a tool to break down barriers. My community needs to know they are valuable people who deserve a better quality of life. I would like to continue my education by enrolling in a Leadership and Nation Building program, so I can provide a civics program for my community. I would also like to apply for a Chamiza Grant to conduct a survey in our community so our tribal leadership will support the people through mutual love and respect. The Preamble in the Constitution of the Zuni Tribe states, "to encourage and promote all movements and efforts leading to the general welfare of our tribe" (Constitution of the Zuni Tribe, 1970, p. 1). I would like to continue honoring the voices of our ancestors who held only the highest regard for a prosperous life for all.

Reference

Constitution of the Zuni Tribe. (1970). Retrieved from www.ashiwi.org/Documents/RevisedZuniConstitutionAnnotatedFinal.pdf

Part 2

Working With and Within

6 Heritage Seeds in Preschool

Engaging Elders

Norene Lonasee

My name is Norene Lonasee; I'm from the pueblo of Zuni. My clans are Corn and child of the Turkey clan. I have lived in Zuni all my life and work for the Pueblo of Zuni Head Start as a teacher assistant. I have three sons and one daughter, and I live with my husband. Growing up I was always surrounded by my extended family members, even though at home there was only my parents and my sister living on White Rock Road.

I spoke the Zuni language until I was about in the second grade, and then I started speaking English. At the time I didn't get much practice speaking English due to most of my family members and friends only speaking Zuni. When speaking English, I used to speak it backward, until one day in class a classmate asked me if I was speaking backward. Then she started laughing and making fun of me in front of our peers. From then on I did my best to learn the English language.

I think it was about the same time I had made up my mind to be a teacher, just so I could help others. I remember thinking about what my grandparents and great grandparents were teaching me: *We, the younger ones, are to grow up to be the ones to care for the elderly and speak for them, and in return teach our young to do the same for us when we get older.* I was very fortunate to have grown up surrounded by my elders, who lived the old ways without much influence from mainstream America. Life was taken at a slower pace and connected to nature and to our ancestors through daily prayer and showing respect to all living spirits that surround us. Much of their teachings were spiritual, which has guided me in my life's journey.

As a teacher, my dreams are to have a lasting impact on our young Zuni children—to believe in themselves to achieve goals in education, as well as continue to carry on the language, culture, traditions, and the beautiful Zuni heritage that they are born into, and then pass this on to their children. My dream is also to become a good instructor of our Zuni language and culture—to help maintain and pass on the Zuni values, morals, and teachings that my great-grandparents spoke of when they spoke of their elders. My hopes are to develop teaching tools and materials to make learning the Zuni language fun and easy. In part of my journey on teaching the Zuni language and cultural to our children, as the elders always would tell me,

> Believe and pray each morning for what you really want to do; if the *Nanakwe* hear your prayers, you may be granted with whatever you ask for. If it is good, the Nanakwe will help you on your way to what you want, only believe in them and yourself. Always look to where you are going.

As in any journey, there are obstacles. On my journey to obtain my Associate Degree in Early Childhood Multicultural Education, I was running into obstacles in math concepts, and I needed financial assistance for tuition and books. But just when I started to believe that my goal to reach that degree started to fade, I saw a flyer about ZETAC helping teachers continue with their studies to graduate. For me, this was the very thing I was praying for. At this point in time, I was starting to lack confidence in myself as a student, and I was concerned about paying for college. I had been pawning my silver and turquoise jewelry to pay for my tuition, books, child care, and gas to travel to and from Gallup for classes. Each semester I did the same thing by taking out all my pawns, just so I would have it to pawn again next semester. From the start I always felt ZETAC was what I was looking for—the answer to my problems. With the financial assistance, proper guidance, and support from ZETAC, I have accomplished my goal of earning my associate degree in early childhood multicultural education.

My first event was the first ZETAC Summer Institute with Project-Based Learning. That summer we did our first *Dream Town* and worked on what we wanted for our Zuni children. We collaborated on ideas, dreams, and wishes for our Zuni children and community. As we worked on our Dream Town, I felt we all had about the same ideas of what our community needed to support our Zuni children in living a good, productive life. Everybody had the same dreams. It was a collaboration of ideas of how much more beautiful our community would be if we were just more aware of each other's feelings and thoughts That summer, I learned a great deal about how others felt about our children and our community, along with the importance of keeping the language, culture, traditions, and beliefs. I felt uplifted, with renewed energy about teaching in general. I also found the support that I truly needed to continue on in achieving my goal of obtaining a Bachelor's Degree in education.

My project was *The Zuni Heirloom Seed Project*. I had the opportunity provide Zuni heirloom seeds to Head Start children and families to plant in the school garden and at their homes. The seeds that I provided to my students are seeds that I have been collecting for over 20 years. The collection of seeds goes back to the teaching of the Zuni elders of how seeds are precious to the Zuni people. The Zuni world of prayers and giving blessings revolves around seeds and rain that leads to having a good long life. So I try to continue to live in the same manner as the old ones. I have been collecting these seeds from my own family gardens and from the Zuni community.

My hopes are to have families start they own family gardens that contains no Genetically Modified Organisms (GMOs). Part of the teaching is for families to start small gardens at home with some germinated and dry seeds, then save some of the seeds from harvested plants to start their own Zuni heirloom seed collections at home to continue the path that was been set for us.

The Zuni Heirloom Seed Project started with teaching the children at Zuni Head Start about planting various seeds, as I was implementing more of the Zuni culture and traditions related to planting. The families of the children wanted to learn more about traditional gardening. The lessons include traditional stories of the Zuni people about their values of the seeds, rain, and good harvest, which is also spoken of in blessings of a long, prosperous life.

Included in the Zuni Heirloom Seed Project were the stories and lessons on the importance of corn. Corn has always been vital to the Zuni people, since the time of emergence from the four underworlds. To help the children understand that there were different colors of the corn, and the order of the corn sisters and their representations of the cardinal directions, I introduced songs in the Zuni language to the children. The songs help children to learn to identify colors and directions in the Zuni language. Within the Zuni culture, traditions, and religion, corn is present in one form or another throughout a Zuni person's life. A newborn is washed with an ear of corn and presented within the fourth day of life to guide and protect the infant in starting his or her journey in life. The ear of corn that is given to the baby by the paternal grandmother and aunts is to bless the infant with a long life and to protect the infant from the spirits and bad dreams, since at the time of birth to about age four children are seen as raw beings, who are considered pure spirit beings who can still communicate and see into the spirit world. Therefore the corn is given to help guide the infant, and the ear of corn is considered as a spiritual mother for the child. Then throughout a Zuni person's life, corn is used for various purposes: Corn is one of the main ingredient in Zuni meals. Corn meal is sprinkled each morning along with a morning prayer or in other religious activities. Finally, corn is used to prepare the body on the final journey to the Zuni heavens.

The Zuni Heirloom Seed Project includes other seeds, such beans, squash, melons, chili, and other vegetables. When starting the lesson on gardening,

I provide the dark, rich soil that has been collected from the nearby forest areas or arroyos after a heavy rainfall, to be used as potting soil and in garden beds. Next we germinate some of the seeds using paper towels and plastic bags. Children pick from various colored corn seeds and beans to be placed within the folds of paper towels. Each of the folded paper towels is sprinkled with water and placed in clear plastic baggie, then taped on the window. As children are germinating their seeds in bags, I tell them of how they are like parents now to watch, care for, and talk to their seeds each day, so that the seeds will be willing to thrive and grow into tall, strong plants. As the seeds grow in various stages of growth, I name each of the stages in Zuni and explain the changes that are occurring in the growing plant.

Some of my favorite memories are of children getting off the bus in the morning saying, "Good morning, how are you?" to the plants. Then after school before boarding their busses, the children would look over the fence to talk to their plants. Before leave they would say, "*De'wani*" (tomorrow).

The other half of the project is on learning about the types of soil to use when gardening in Zuni. Since Zuni is in a dry, desert area with little rain, and with the climate changing it seems like shorter planting seasons. Knowing the soil and when to start planting is very important. I include the techniques and teachings of our Zuni elders on how to create waffle gardens, or create circular depressions in garden beds to collect rain water, or just to retain the water within close proximity of the plants. With the lesson on gardening, I include the lessons on the water cycle and the importance of conserving water. When teaching young children lessons on gardening, I include the with the cycle of plants, the water cycle, respect for Mother Earth and a "Greener World," along with stories and teachings of how gardening is important in all cultures around the world.

With the Zuni Heirloom Seed Project, the collected seeds contain no GMOs and are not from packaged seed envelopes. The seeds that I have collected are seeds that were found stored in jars, old coffee cans, or in old abandon kitchen draws sitting in old farming houses in old Zuni farming villages. One batch of seeds was found within a wall in an old adobe house. When elders found out my intentions for the seeds, the elders began giving me some of their seeds too. These seeds also came along with family stories. Some stories included why they saved the seeds, either for the sweetness of the fruit, the color, the size, or that the seeds had been saved by their own elders. I share some of the stories of their bountiful harvests, happiness, sharing of crops, and plenty of humorous stories of long ago of families' uniting, of coming together to work and pray as one. The stories of praying for rain in the dry desert country and receiving their blessings, which also created blessings of another, the hard work of repairing washed-out roads during the monsoon seasons to get to their gardens in the farming villages to save their crops they had worked very hard for.

The elders talking about working together as families is something I treasure most. The ideas of people working together, helping, teaching, and learning from each other make our world would be a better place. As a participant of ZETAC, I truly feel the togetherness of teachers gathering to learn, share ideas, and teach one another, so we as teachers guide our students to a higher level of thinking using the Zuni language, culture, traditions, values, and morals.

I am so grateful for having had the opportunity to be a ZETAC participant from the beginning. The knowledge that each individual brought and shared empowered all those who were there. It took people from the outside to come in to help us in Zuni know what we wanted for our children and for our community. From this ZETAC experience I will remember the people, the ideas, and the hopes and dreams for our children in retaining the Zuni culture and language moving on into the future. I appreciate the two ladies who came to Zuni, and I believe it was our ancestors who sent them into our lives to empower us in our own ways. Each and every one of us learned something; we took something, and we used it to make it better somewhere else: with our schools, our community, and even our families.

ZETAC has had an impact on the Zuni community. The dreams and visions that the participants drew on the Dream Town posters are becoming a reality in our Zuni community; I see the improvements being made. ZETAC empowered us and gave a stronger voice to the teaching community to bring more awareness for our Zuni community on issues that concern our students and families. Most importantly more Zuni language, culture, traditions, and the Zuni Core Values are being taught in the Zuni schools. ZETAC has taught us many techniques on teaching and how to motivate students, but it also showed us ways to bring awareness to issues and better our community as well. I will be forever grateful for having been a participant of ZETAC; I have a better understanding of the teaching world, *Elahkwa*.

7 Western Science and Zuni Language, Culture, and History

Ray Hartwig

As I sit here writing my contribution to this book, I am planning my fifth Project-Based Learning (PBL) endeavor examining Zuni land and water resources, aimed at sophomore Earth Science students. First, I received approval from district supervisory personnel after writing an email entitled: *Nine Reasons Why We Should Do This Project.* I have listed those nine reasons below.

1) The students get to use multi-function water testing units in real life situations.
2) The students become familiar with use of GPS devices and maps in the field.
3) We get to identify wildlife in natural habitats.
4) If we bring fourth graders with us, sophomores get exposed to mentoring/teaching practices.
5) We get to involve local experts and technicians showing students their work with Bureau of Indian Affairs (BIA) Forestry, Department of Natural Resources Hydrology and Wildlife Management. This can also lead to exposure to possible career options for the students' future.
6) I am able to tie together 21st-century science practices with Zuni history and culture by bringing along a cultural leader who describes the importance of water to the Zuni people throughout history and speaks to them of their cultural heritage regarding Zuni ancient dwelling sites.
7) I am coordinating with the tenth-grade English/Language Arts (ELA) and Social Science departments to integrate their curricula and make it a multi-departmental venture.
8) All of the students and their parents (that I have talked to) are completely behind this project and support it without exception.
9) It requires very little in terms of district resources, really just local transportation and four hours of bus driver wages 12 times.

The return message read, "Okay, sounds good. How can we help?"

Second, I visited the Tribal Administrator/Conservation department head and the Zuni Conservation department hydrologist to work out a calendar schedule. I then verified this schedule with the Zuni High School principal. Third, I contacted my Zuni cultural advisor and grade level colleagues to plan their curricula for this five-week project. I am now in the process of filling out my travel request forms for all 12 trips for the approval of District Transportation. The project will begin on October 16 and the individual student presentations will end Thanksgiving week. I have to admit this process gets easier every year...

How is a sixth year, Level Two Licensed, high school science instructor able to put something like this together? *This* is the story I would like to tell.

I

I have lived approximately 30 miles from the Zuni Pueblo for 30 years. My connections with the Zuni people and their art have existed nearly as long. After my children grew up and moved to Albuquerque to attend college, I realized something was missing in my life. When I was 18 years old, my father died; I was the eldest of seven children. While attending college in the 1970s, eventually acquiring degrees in Philosophy and Biology, I was cast in the role of stand-in father and mentor to my siblings. When they grew up and went their separate ways (we are all still very close), I moved to New Mexico. I married my best friend and helped to raise her two children from a previous marriage. We had two children of our own, mentioned above, whom I love dearly. It didn't take a great deal of contemplation to discover what had changed in my life that left me feeling empty. *Where were the kids?*

My wife JoHanna, who was an elementary school teacher at the time, suggested that perhaps I would like to try my hand at being a substitute teacher, just to see if I would like it. It was a blast! I was a long-term substitute for seven or eight years teaching in the Gallup-McKinley and Zuni Public School systems. After a friend of mine, who happened to be vice principal at Zuni High School (ZHS), observed me teaching U.S. government and economics to ZHS seniors, he said that he had a proposition for me. He offered that if I followed the New Mexico path to alternative licensure known as *OPAL*, the Online Portfolio Alternative License, he would hire me at any school in which he was an administrator. Two years later I had a full-time position teaching Earth science at Zuni High School, where he was then principal.

After my first year of teaching on a permanent, full-time basis, I was nearly a beaten man. This was hard work! I heard an announcement on the P.A. at the end of that first school year that representatives from the University of New Mexico College of Education were setting up a professional development organization known as ZETAC. They would provide summertime workshops in project-based learning (PBL) and traditional Zuni teaching and learning models. The opportunity also existed to receive scholarships for further educational training at the UNM College of Education. Though I was still two years away from submitting my OPAL Level One certification portfolio, I knew that eventually I would need a Master's Degree to reach Level Three licensure. More importantly, I knew that I needed additional training and ideas to serve the students I was instructing more effectively. I thought, *Why not? Let's see what they have to say.* That afternoon I met with the ZETAC coordinators. I can't remember much of what they had to say, but I do remember thinking that it was *do-able.* I was desperate to find methods that would enable me to truly reach the Zuni 16-year-olds under my care, thereby achieving a greater level of mutual self-fulfillment and satisfaction. This was the beginning of ZETAC and the turning point in my career as an educator.

II

Nobody knows for sure how long the Zuni people have lived in the isolated enclave of west-central New Mexico they call *The Middle Place.* Certainly it has been many hundreds of years and perhaps much longer. I won't attempt to retell their tribulations since the appearance of the first Europeans in the late 1500s. The key to their survival has been adherence to their *core values,* which include mutual respect, brotherhood, and cooperation.

The Zuni had no written version of their language until the late 20th century. For thousands of years, all communication was verbal. They taught each other through *demonstration* and practice. Those Zuni who did something well, whether it was winnowing wheat, making productive gardens that needed little water, or making arrowheads, taught those who wanted to do it well. They taught and learned between generations. The tribal elders passed on their knowledge to younger Zuni adults, who taught in turn the children, who practiced the activities necessary for life in the arid southwestern United States.

III

I was told that Mr. Lewis, then superintendent of Zuni Public Schools, wanted to develop an organization that would try to achieve three major goals. The first was to incorporate traditional Zuni teaching models into classrooms in the district. The second was to reintroduce *Zuni Core Values* as part of the teaching curricula, thereby making Zuni culture and history a larger part of everyday classroom practice at all grade levels. The third goal was to make it possible for members of the community who wanted to be a part of the education process in Zuni to do so—to provide scholarship opportunities, in conjunction with the UNM College of Education, for new Zuni educational assistants and certified instructors. This was ZETAC: Zuni Engaging Teachers and Community.

The first workshops were held in the summer of 2013. I consider myself fortunate to have attended that, and all subsequent workshops, offered. One might ask why this was such a different professional development experience. I must admit, that first year, I asked myself the same question. This was to be my time to recuperate from a first challenging school year after all. To begin with, we learned in-depth perspectives of Zuni culture and history. We toured ancient dwelling sites in the company of cultural and religious leaders from the tribe as part of our activities. After living and working with Zuni community members and artisans for over 20 years, I was surprised at how much I learned.

The second week of workshop events transitioned to PBL. Remarkably competent experts in the field facilitated these workgroups. At the end of this program, each of us was challenged to develop a project that we could use the following school year in our classes. I reluctantly agreed, thinking to myself that this would be another layer of work I would have to plan for and execute without any degree of confidence in the outcome. I did do it, however. After all, I promised that I would. It wasn't nearly as difficult an endeavor as I had imagined. It was hard to gage the positive effects on my students. I was bolstered by the experience and shared my progress that spring in a March ZETAC workshop.

The encouragement I received from my mentors (the ZETAC coordinators and instructors) was so uplifting that I immediately planned another project involving my geology class for the end of the school year. This project was planned to connect the science of mineralogy and the ancient Zuni art form of fetish carving. I felt that this project, too, had real potential and worked on ideas that would make it better the following year.

I describe below the planning and execution of these projects and their evolution over the next few years. The point I would like to share here, though, is the unexpected ease I experienced when constructing these activities. This is partly because the subjects I teach readily lend themselves to outdoor investigation (it *is* Earth Science, after all). I believe it is also because of the intimate connection the Zuni students feel for this Middle Place, the unique *sense of place* they are so privileged to be a part of, as their blood relatives have over the thousand(s) of years past.

IV

I believe an endeavor like this book and my chapter in it is only really useful to the extent that it can help other educators reproduce similar results. It is important in this age of standardized testing, teacher summative evaluations, and never-ending (and sometimes conflicting) directives from state public education departments to be able to construct something *real* that both equips our students with the tools our society requires from them in adult life *and* does so in a way that maximizes those transcendent moments we all cherish as teacher/students and student/teachers. With this in mind, I will walk through the process I used in my first few projects, how I subsequently modified them, and finally, the insights these efforts led me to realize as an educator.

While there may be a certain art in selecting projects, for a science teacher living in New Mexico the environment in which we live is abundant with possibility. Teaching in the arid climes of Zuni as an Earth Science teacher, it is understandable that issues concerning water come to mind. The rich cultural history of the Zuni people should inspire a social science instructor to develop themes close to their curricula. Even urban areas of the state are only a short bus ride away from interesting geological and historical venues; however, one just needs to be open to the options.

After choosing to focus on surface and ground water resources, I felt my first move was to involve local experts. This led to a series of meetings with members of the Zuni Department of Natural Resources and Conservation Department. Viewing the raw footage of these meetings years later is actually rather humorous (it's always a good idea to document first steps for later contemplation and revision). I was asking them for ideas, and it appeared they were stoically sitting there wondering how much extra work I was trying to get them to do. In the event, I was able to get commitments from the hydrologist and the GPS/GIS expert. The Fish and Wildlife representative declined, and Environmental and Forestry technicians said they might be interested if I could make a proposal that interested them.

That first project was in the winter. I had the assistance of an ELA colleague of mine. I also had the help of the Zuni hydrologist and the GPS/GIS coordinator. It was a simple project; we did water quality testing at four locations, learned how water levels are measured, and gathered information on the watersheds. Over the following few years I learned of springs feeding the lakes and which surface water resources were ephemeral. We worked with GPS locating equipment and expanded our awareness of the utility of GIS in rural locations like Zuni. Something was missing, though, and it was the history and culture of the Zuni people.

I have always viewed the science I've taught in Zuni as being intimately connected with the history and rich culture of the Zuni people. The role that the unique topography of the Colorado Plateau has played in the history of the Zuni people after the Europeans appeared, is well-documented in the historical record. The sacred places like *Dowa Yalanne Mesa*, Sacred Springs, and Gallestina Canyon, among others, play an important part in the Zuni yearly cycle of religious observations, in addition to presenting a very special geological perspective.

I wanted the participation of local cultural and religious leaders to share this view with my 16-year-old students. I am not exactly sure why this has been so difficult. Now in my fifth year of this project, I am hoping to bring in two religious leaders. If successful it will be the third time we have been able to add this crucial component. There is a disconnect between today's teenagers and the traditional Zuni lifestyle, to be sure. This makes a renewed association with the land, the students, and their history and language all the more important.

V

Last year we added another important aspect of Zuni traditional instruction, that being *inter-generational teaching/learning*. By bringing along all of the fourth-grade classes of Shiwi Ts'ana Elementary School on our field trips, high school sophomores were exposed to the mentoring process so prevalent throughout Zuni history. We chose fourth grade because they are the elementary grade level, which is assessed in science by the state of New Mexico. A month ago I saw a former Shiwi Ts'ana instructor who now works as a district coordinator for Teach for America. She shared a survey with me completed after last year's project, which showed uniformly higher scores in fourth grade standardized science tests than in previous years.

Another change in the project design for this year is the individual research projects each student selects as part of each fieldtrip. The students have chosen subjects such as: erosion, soil composition, water quality, rock and mineral testing, algae and lichen identification, insect identification, tree and sagebrush identification, and invasive species. This encourages them to *own* what they do in the field and to stay focused on their objectives.

This was the first and most important of the projects we designed at Zuni High School. Over the last five years this water quality project has impacted the greatest number of students. It has placed scientific instruments into the hands of 16-year-old science students in real environments with real self-chosen objectives. It has reached out and touched elementary students and formed bonds between two generations of Zuni youth that will last a lifetime. This project has also demonstrated to Earth science students the connection between what they study in their textbooks and their cultural heritage in this very special part of the Southwest. Perhaps most importantly, it has renewed their vision of a sense of *place* and *belonging* that that belongs to them alone.

VI

The success of this project encouraged me to develop others. It is a different kind of teaching; it was more wide open and fun. All teachers know that when our students are happy, our job is a joy to perform. Not every activity in the Earth Science and Geology curriculum is based on a PBL model. There are writing, and quizzes, and lab exercises, the usual science stuff. But the promise of being in the field on a cool fall morning listening to birds and sketching geological formations or collecting insects, tree specimens, or clay to be used in their pottery classes is something my students have grown to look forward to, and it really makes my job easier, because they are happy.

The second big project I designed was for my geology class in mineralogy. It involves learning basic chemistry so that the students can understand how the elements combine to form compounds. They learn the periodic table, electron energy levels, and the different types of chemical bonds. With an understanding of compounds, we examine minerals: the characteristics all minerals have in common, the various ways that minerals can form, and the seven basic classes of minerals. Learning the properties of minerals and how to quantify them in the lab had been interesting to my students, but when the connection between Southwest minerals and the ancient art of Zuni carving occurred to me, I knew I was onto a hot idea. Why not take the minerals we had tested and let an accomplished Zuni fetish artist show the students the traditional fetish carving art form?

To tie this project into our mineralogy curriculum and to improve writing communication skills, I asked every student participating to write a two-page paper every week describing how they thought the tests we had done on mineral properties were reflected in their experience carving those minerals. We used calcium fluoride (fluorite), the silicate mineral serpentine, the metamorphic rock "Picasso marble," and many other minerals used by Zuni carvers. We then tested the minerals/rocks for density, hardness, streak, luster, the acid test for the presence of calcium carbonate, crystal form, and fracture/cleavage. Over the course of several weeks, they were able to try various samples and the students' understanding of how the results of these tests altered their experience carving became progressively more detailed and profound. This project *did* require some capital outlay for grinding wheels, Dremel drills with attachments, and buffing wheels. These expenditures amounted to approximately $2,000 and were subsidized by the ZETAC grant spoken of earlier.

In the end it was a rewarding experience for most students, as many have relatives who carve fetishes, which they sell as part of their income. Some students assist those relatives in collecting samples, and some already had a degree of carving experience. Some students asked if they could bring their own mineral/rock samples. There were students from previous geology classes asked if they could participate in this project again, after school. It was a project that really did seem to deeply connect with my students in a way even I didn't foresee initially.

VII

Watching the respect the students had for the Zuni elders and fetish carvers I brought into my classroom, and sometimes accompanied us in the field, increased my desire to expand the *inter-generational teaching/learning* (I-G T/L) model used previously by incorporating the fourth graders into the Zuni Lakes Project described above. To this end, I asked the assistance of one of my PBL mentors. Was she aware of an elementary school teacher, somewhere in the Eastern part of the country, who might be interested in having some of my students present a lesson on local geology to his/her class via Skype? She then set me up with a first-grade teacher in Ohio who was teaching a unit on Native Peoples. Because of the time difference, my students would have to log on at 7:00 a.m. local time. I made this project optional, for extra credit, and several of my geology students wanted to participate.

In the event, as I was having my students prepare lesson plans on the geologic history of Dowa Yalanne (D-Y) Mesa, a very surprising phenomena occurred. Some of my students asked if they could instead speak of the role D-Y Mesa played in Zuni history. When I agreed, other students asked if they could present how D-Y Mesa figured into their creation and migration story. There were also students who wanted to show their artwork of Dowa Yalanne to these first graders. Of course, I agreed to all of these ideas.

As I did so, I started contemplating what was happening to my geology class. You see, for me the class was only about what *I* had taught, which was the geologic history of D-Y Mesa forming over the three periods of the Mesozoic Era. It was apparent that my students viewed this sacred place in a much more holistic and complex way.

While my students continued to prepare and later offer their views to the first-grade class in Ohio, I had time to continue to think about what had happened and what it might mean to how I could reach my students. The presentation went well, and I could tell was great fun for the members of my class who participated. In addition, the first-grade students were very active participants in the streaming event and later sent very cute pictures of the projects they did in their Native Peoples unit that were inspired by the affair. This experience taught me something much more far-reaching, however.

VIII

I had a series of discussions with one of my colleagues, a Zuni ELA instructor. We spoke of a model that was taking shape in my contemplations, which was very dissimilar to the linear paradigm taught in most Western classrooms. Instead of parsing each item in my state standards, building from one idea to the next in a very logical and straightforward fashion, I began to apprehend that my students didn't necessarily live in this type of world:

> Based on this perspective, the first way of thinking and knowing has to do with one's physical place. That is, one has to come to terms with where one physically lives. One has to know one's home, one's village, and then the land, the earth upon which one lives. These are the hills, canyons, valleys, forests, mountains, streams, rivers, plains, deserts, lakes, and seas—the place where you live, awareness of your physical environment.
>
> (Heidlebaugh, 1985, as cited in Cajete, 1994, p. 47)

Most of my Zuni students didn't see Dowa Yalanne Mesa as a free-standing mesa formed on a base of Triassic Period mudstone—layers of sand forming dunes on what is now the Colorado Plateau portion of the Southwest when it was in the western part of the single continent of Pangaea. During the break-up of Pangaea later in the Jurassic Period, approximately 200 million years ago, this area was repeatedly under water which allowed the sediments forming the bulk of D-Y to be deposited, compacted, and cemented into the layers we see today.

My students see something entirely different. They see the home of their War-Gods, and they see the dreams they have had about D-Y. When they look at D-Y they remember what they were taught about the role it played as a citadel against the attacks by the Spanish in the 17th century. They might remember the stories they were told by relatives who climbed the mesa when they were young and saw or heard things that stayed with them for the rest of their lives. Many of my students think of the Great Deluge and how a Zuni Rain Priest sent his son and daughter into the water surrounding D-Y to make the flood-waters subside. Most of my students have drawn or painted representations of Dowa Yalanne, not necessarily as an assignment for art class but as a reminder or perhaps a gift to a loved one, *because it is so important*. This is not only how they view D-Y but the entire world, with themselves at the center and everything that they have experienced being a part of their place in this world.

In thinking about these concepts holistically, I began incorporating this model into my geology class, which allows my students to experience the science classroom as they do their reality outside of the classroom. We do more artwork in geology now. We look at a large topographic map of the Zuni Reservation, which I have mounted on the wall, and try to interpret its features not only from a viewpoint of geological processes at work but in light of their creation story. This is not only more appealing to the students because of its relevance to their daily lives and "highest thoughts," it also leads to a more creative perspective for me as a teacher.

For years I had looked at the most prominent topographic feature on this, which is invisible from a ground level view: Gallestina Canyon. One afternoon one of my students asked if the Great Deluge, an important part of the Zuni creation story, might really have happened. The artist's representations they had seen showed water surrounding D-Y Mesa. I thoughtfully looked at the map in the back of the class and saw Gallestina Canyon as if for the first time, and said, "I can't say for sure how, or when, or even if an event like the Flood you are asking about occurred, but look at the topo map in the back. I *do* know there is only one kind of geologic force that can create a structure like Gallestina Canyon. Do you know what that force is?"

Of course the entire class responded, "Water!"

I agreed with them and asked them to look at where the opening of Gallestina Canyon was oriented and once again, responding almost in unison, they said, "It is aimed right at D-Y Mesa!"

After this I began to look at their stories, artwork, and dreams not as just a useful adjunct to a differentiated curriculum but as their perspective of *life itself*. Asking them to write about potential interactions with their younger cousins and siblings, in story form, about scientific ideas they were being exposed to or thought they understood, has become a regular part of my weekly efforts to support our school's literacy enhancement efforts. A whole new panorama of possible instructional strategies appears when one is willing to look at science, the world, and life through this more experiential model *of place*.

IX

I often describe to those of my colleagues who ask about the process of reconciling the state and Common Core Standards with my concept of PBL and I-G T/L thusly: "Rip up the State Standards into little pieces and throw them on the floor."

They shudder. Then I tell them,

Now paste each of these pieces onto the framework of a beautiful and creative project that you and your students have imagined and then designed after the likeness of something that is precious to you. It does not matter where they fit or how they overlap. It does not matter if what once came before now comes after. You will find when you are done, not only are all the little pieces gone from the floor but there is room left on your beautiful creation to attach lessons of joy and wonder.

It is bit over the top I admit but it demonstrates a good point. Most of the colleagues I have worked with over the years are creative. They are blessed with an artistry and ingenuity that is all too often crushed by the perceived weight of the K-12 State Standards Manual. This perception is also all too often reinforced by building administrators carrying around a teacher observation checklist in one hand and the latest state school assessment printout in their back pocket. "The authoritative leader is a visionary; he motivates people by making clear to them how their work fits into a larger vision for the organization" (Goleman, 2000, p. 83).

In principle, the importance of these techniques, and others like them, for Native American learners has been described since the early 1990s. Goin (1999), Hankes (1996), and Pewewardy (1998), to name but a few, have all emphasized the differences in Native language registers, the concept of time, and the importance of silence and visual imagery in Native American instructional models.

I deeply respect my colleagues at Zuni High School. I have also noticed on more than one occasion that factors such as lack of support (leadership and financial), low socio-economic standing of the community in which they teach, low standardized test scores, and a seeming ambivalence of state and district education policies, have left my colleagues somewhat at a loss for discerning ways of achieving positive outcomes for our students. This is completely sensible from my point of view. It can oftentimes seem that government policies (starting in Washington, D.C., and running down through state and local levels) have to be changed before change is possible in our own backyard, and we all know that isn't going to happen any time soon. Certain suggestions I have made regarding the efficacy and "do-ability" of PBL principles in even the most fundamental of ways have been responded to by listing the circumstances and forces that are arrayed against accomplishing any kind of lasting success in the classroom.

1)   I don't have enough time to plan some big project.

Do bits and pieces as you do have time. Look for support from interested parents and community members. Call local experts/technical people to help you brainstorm ideas. Share the load with colleagues. Make the planning part of your daily classroom activities with the students engaging in support and discussion.

2) There is no way I can get through my entire curriculum if I do something like this.

    Make this your curriculum. Populate your project with all of the points that need to be covered. You are doing your curriculum, just in another fashion than that to which you are accustomed. It is a new way that perhaps will involve your students more deeply and wouldn't that be nice?

3) It would never be approved by Central Office.

    How can you possibly know that if you don't try? This is the wave of the future; many schools are incorporating PBL as part of district policy. Get in front of the curve!

4) Oh great, I have to do everything I am doing now and something like this too? Typical!

    This IS what you are doing and all that you are doing, if you do it correctly and with student involvement. Get excited once again about your chosen profession!

I serve a district where over 80% of the community lives below the poverty line and I have seen that PBL and I-G T/L can make a difference.

X

In five short years I have gone from a Pre-Level I, first-year instructor (unsure as to whether I wanted to be a second-year instructor) to a highly effective, Level II, Science Department chair, one year away from a master's degree in educational leadership from UNM. Of course, the *willingness* to undergo a reboot of my perspective on education had to come from within. The framework that enabled this willingness to blossom into a *new life* in education I must say is due to my dear friends and mentors listed below, under the aegis of ZETAC. My affection and gratitude toward the ZETAC coordinators and instructors and toward all of my fellow ZETAC colleagues can't be adequately expressed in words, but they know how I feel. The real winners in all of our efforts (you know what I am going to say) of course are the 70–80, 16-year-old, Zuni young men and women who move through my classes every year. It is to them that I dedicate this chapter, for without their companionship on our shared voyage of teaching/learning and learning/teaching my life would be much poorer.

References

Cajete, G. (1994). *Look to the mountain: An ecology of Indigenous education.* Durango, CO: Kivaki Press.

Goleman, D. (2000). Leadership that gets results. *Harvard Business Review, 78*(2), 78–90.

Goin, L. (1999, June). *Planning academic programs for American Indian success: Learning strategies workshop.* Indigenous education around the world: Workshop papers from the World Indigenous People's Conference, Albuquerque, NM.

Hankes, J. E. (1996). *Investigating the correspondence between native American pedagogy and constructivist-based instruction.* Paper presented at the annual convention of the American Educational Research Association, New York. (ERIC Document Reproduction Service No. ED401086).

Pewewardy, C. D. (1998). *Culturally responsive teaching for American Indian learners.* Paper presented at the Kansas Institute on Effective Teaching Practices for Indian Education, Lawrence, KS. (ERIC Document Reproduction Service No. ED459981).

8 Colors of Corn

My Story of Infusing Indigenous Culture into My High School English Class

Joy Cushman

My name is Joy. I am the child of no tribe. Yet, if I could assign my parents to clans, I would be the child of a non-profit manager and an educator. I am the oldest of four children and was raised in a home where some of the greatest teachings were to work, serve others, read books, go outside to play, and to remember "we don't have money for that." I don't remember understanding or learning about race, ethnicity, or skin-color from my parents. My father said he came from "white trash"; that was the closest to racial identification that I understood. I would grow up in communities divided by race but not understand why. Anyone who has learned or researched cultural privilege will understand how there are both benefits and detriments to this kind of "colorblindness." It wasn't until high school and college that I began to understand and experience racial conflict for myself.

To understand all else, one must understand that I am a White, married, middle-aged woman living and teaching on a Native American Pueblo reservation in New Mexico. I was not born here or even in this state. I did not specifically set out to teach among Indigenous people, nor did I arrive with strong cultural bias or determined activism. Instead, I had to learn what being White meant and how to be a White woman in a Native land. I had to own up to my own pre-conceptions about Native American peoples, reservations, the history of Indigenous peoples in America (and worldwide), and confront my own ignorance, cynicism, shortsightedness, and narrow-minded thinking. These things being said, I did not arrive in Zuni to teach *feeling* like I stereotyped people or harbored prejudice. Instead, I had to confront my own cultural identity, open myself to being teachable from people around me, be willing to re-educate myself in a myriad of ways, and partake in critical conversations, many of which were difficult or uncomfortable.

I have learned much since my arrival in Zuni, especially about the importance of re-examining my own identity in reference to my cultural background, heritage, beliefs, identity, and privilege. I have also had to learn about and try to understand generational trauma, alcoholism, poverty, diabetes, abandonment, language loss, colonialism, White privilege, and historical perspective. I also have learned to be prepared with strong emotions and expect that I may not be welcome. All physical locations on the reservation are open to outsiders, and even though I have lived in Zuni for over six years, ceremonies (even those taking place in open air) are not available for watching or participation, or that all subjects regarding these events are open for discussion. I understand this, but I did have to learn it. I also learned not to expect Native American youth to act, dress, or necessarily speak differently than the average child or teenager.

I have always loved traveling to new places and learning about people and cultures. It is fitting then that I would choose to move to Zuni or that Zuni would choose me. When someone begins teaching in Zuni schools, the first thing students ask is "Why did you move to Zuni?" My classes were a bit dumbfounded when I explained that I *chose* Zuni. I wasn't placed here (like with Teach for America) or raised near here (in Gallup, Grants, or Ramah and found nearby employment). I didn't even choose to teach here as a last option. I applied all over New Mexico, interviewed all over New Mexico, even received job offerings from several schools in New Mexico; however, when I came to Zuni to interview, I *knew* I was meant to be here.

My husband and I drove the three hours from Albuquerque, New Mexico, to Zuni and I remember the beauty of the red rock mesas and the drive from Grants up Route 53. I remember passing the first vestiges of spring visible on the large grove of cottonwood trees in the Bosque and then coming into view of Dowa Yalanne Mesa—the Great Corn Mesa. It truly is breathtaking. When we turned in to park for my interview, I remember my happiness seeing the globe willow trees that stand before the high school. They are my favorite trees in the southwestern United States. Chartreuse, with early spring leaves, they swayed in the breeze. I felt it was a sign.

There are amazing benefits of living far away from a city. There is negligible noise or light pollution. Twelve months of the year I can see the Milky Way at night and the air is pristine. I am not tempted by fast-food, take-out, drive-through, or delivery. Traffic is a way of the past (except after home football games), and I don't have to wait for the light to change. Overall, I feel life is simpler and more meaningful, just also more distanced from what I know to be a standard American life.

I would remember feeling that this high school was "just the right size" (at 400 students) as opposed to the enormous high school (5,000 students) from which I graduated. I liked the feeling I had there, in the community, and when shown the apartment I would live in later. Before we left, my husband and I got gasoline, and a woman remarked on my frog purse. She told us that there was a "Frog Clan," and again, I felt that part of me belonged with these kind, good-natured people. My husband and I also asked where we could hike safely. I knew that if I had access to wilderness and nature that I wouldn't be lonely or bored, even if Zuni was remote or isolated in terms of businesses.

Upon accepting a teaching position, and not being a tribal member, my family moved into a *teacherage*, as the next closest place to live is 23 miles away. As a non-tribal member, I can never own land on the reservation. I can never own property or a house here, and thus we do not own our apartment in the teacherage. I rent it specifically for the terms the school district appoints. If the district determines not to employ me, they can evict me and my family.

Zuni is a community unlike any other in which I have lived. Growing up my family was always involved in the community. But Zuni is different. For starters, I cannot hold a seat on the school board, on city or municipal councils, or even event-planning committees because I am not Zuni. I am welcome to attend Tribal Council meetings, but I cannot vote on community issues. My status is like that of a foreigner in another country; I have rights and privileges only as much as a long-term visitor might have. I am fully aware, having read the Pueblo Constitution, that if the tribe were to vote, they could ask all people without tribal status to leave. We understand all of what might be called *limitations*, but we love it here, and our plans are to stay in the Zuni community and teach here for the foreseeable future.

Despite my status on paper in Zuni, my family and I are happy here. I have been warmly welcomed into an organization that has become both a community and force for good of its own accord over the last six years. Developed just over five years ago, in partnership with the University of New Mexico and the W. K. Kellogg Foundation, a group was founded to engage educational leadership development, help provide degrees for Zuni teachers and foster project-based learning in Zuni schools. This group, Zuni: Engaging Teachers and Community (ZETAC), has become a community for me that is positive, inspires change, and helps raise cultural awareness.

I have had so many positive experiences as I have increasingly engaged with both ZETAC members, founders, UNM representatives, and Zuni community members who have shared their rich wisdom and in turn have helped me improve my teaching. As ZETAC members, we get together for professional development, community issues discussions, training on modern issues in teaching, forums on meeting the unique needs of Native students in Zuni, Zuni language classes, and so many more choice opportunities. While these sessions are invaluable, it is the networking and relationships I have developed that I feel I have grown from the most.

I remember at one seminar a man, who was the rain priest, rose to speak. As he spoke, there was a power to his words and a strength and reverent conviction to everything he stated. He shared his deep love for our earth, how he prayed day and night for the land, for the tribe, for the people, for the sky, and for rain. He told us of his sacred duty to fast and make other sacrifices so the tribe would be protected from harm and there would be enough precipitation for the people, that the ancestors would visit through the rain, and that the earth would be filled. Tears streamed down his aged face as he spoke. I remember he talked of weeping at seeing the abuse, disuse, and disinterest young people had for the soil, for the land, and for even caring for their own belongings. He said when he fasted and prayed he could hear loud music booming and rap music and shouting. He shared that he could feel the offense in the spirits of the earth that they couldn't rest even during sacred times. I even remember that he drew parallels between the lakes disappearing, the changes in the weather, and rain patterns with the change in youth, cultural, and tribal habits.

When he spoke, there was perfect silence in the room. In another place, among another group of people, this same man might have been judged for his hair, his appearance, his grammar, but in ZETAC he was respected for his heart, the title, his love and power that exuded from him. His speech was deeply moving to me, so much so that I began paying attention to Zuni cultural seasons and when the sacred times are. When the Zuni people are *de:shkwi* (fasting), I also try to be. I try to follow other facets of observance to respect the tribe and their teachings, their traditions, and their land. I would never have had that experience had I not become a member of ZETAC.

When I accepted the teaching position for which I applied, it ended up being a far cry from the many positions I would fill in for the school district for the next five years. In less than six years I have taught English Intervention, English I, English II, Summer School English, AP English Language and Composition, Algebra I, Algebra II, Trigonometry, ACT Preparation, and Band. I have also sponsored Cheerleading, Dance Club, the Junior Class twice, Pep Band, College Night, and Spirit Club. I have served on district committees, mentored new teachers, and attended (I can't even count how many) professional development sessions. One of the things I have discovered is that in Zuni, you do as you are asked. If there is a need, a job, or a service that needs filling for the community and you are asked, you fill in or find a way. In Anglo-dominated communities they would say "See a need, fill a need"; in Zuni they say, *"Hon ansammo le'na a:dek'yanna"* "We all live accordingly."

This phrase is part of a series of no less than nine tenants called the A:shiwi Core Values. These core values act as guiding principles for Zuni people. They are not laws, rules, or commandments. They are ways of life—of being and thinking. When you consider that the Zuni people have lived on the same land for hundreds, if not thousands, of years without civil wars, without major contentions or conflict, it would make sense that their people would be guided by precepts above basic dos and don'ts.

In my classroom, any conflict, challenge, or trouble can be solved by quoting one of the core values. If a student is disrespectful or insubordinate, I can quote the value, "We will respect one another." If a student has said or done something inappropriate: "We will think before we act and consider the consequences." If students are teasing, bullying, or being unkind: "We will be kind and generous to one another." These core values are one of the ways I try to use the Zuni culture in my classroom regularly. It is a wonderful tool for centering my classroom on the ideals of the Shiwi (Zuni) culture without overstepping my bounds.

I have also worked to learn as much of the Zuni language as I can, and I welcome my students speaking Zuni in my class as well. In Zuni, when a person says "good morning" in the Zuni language, there is a phrase that everyone repeats in unison immediately thereafter. After a few years of teaching in the pueblo and not knowing what was being said, I asked how to say it or *if* I could say it. I finally asked to be taught. It probably took almost half an hour for the Zuni staff to teach the rest of us teachers and administrators what was being said and how to appropriately say it. But it was worth it. Now every time someone says " _____," I can confidently and respectfully respond, "_____." That experience continues to enrich my relationships with community members, staff, students, and families.

I have also found that my ability to say small words or phrases during class can also make a difference. I am now able to tell students to "be quiet," "to listen," "to be respectful," or even the simplest responses like, "yes," and "no." I believe this helps students to know I accept them, their heritage, their language, and their identity. I also display, in my classroom, culturally appropriate educational posters in the Zuni language to reinforce the language. Over time I have learned the alphabet, some basic colors, the names of birds, and more just through studying these Zuni educational posters.

However, I am very challenged when I try to speak the Zuni language. Most Native languages have sounds that are unfamiliar to the English-speaking ear. Sometimes there are vowels, consonants, and blends that are altogether unknown in English. I do my best to try to speak correctly, even when people make fun of my pronunciation. Indigenous language loss is a worldwide plague. There are aspects of Native languages, including Zuni, that as an outsider I am not able to learn; however, I feel welcome as an outsider to try to learn as much as I can.

As a White teacher, a *me:lika* (an outsider), I am encouraged to find as many ways to be culturally sensitive and responsive as possible. I have been told by some that I should not consider teaching Shakespeare because it is so far out of the Native experience and so Eurocentric that it does a disservice to students. On the other hand, I was told during professional development that abstaining from teaching Shakespeare and other European classics is akin to telling students they aren't good enough for college. Ultimately, in the schools, various communities clash as to what is best for the future of the students.

Over the years, I have tried and tested several methods of culturally responsive teaching, but let me share the two I have found the most success with students. The first is finding texts where students relate to the protagonist. Native youth love reading Sherman Alexie. Even if they don't understand everything he is writing about, they love reading him. They understand him; they understand his characters and the feeling of being trapped and torn between two worlds. I know that some of his works have been banned, but I can promise they have never been banned by schools in Native Country. His books are always checked out of the library, and perhaps the only time of the year when I have students *actually read* what we are reading in class is when we read anything by Alexie.

The second strategy I use is to find narratives, biographies, autobiographies, essays, articles, or more written by someone in the tribe (especially by members of the Zuni tribe), and then Native students especially eat it up. The sad truth is that Native literature, by Natives, for Natives (and not just history but stories, legends, fiction) is hard to find. It is easy to find books about Native Americans written by White people or other ethnicities, even well-meaning people. But do the digging to find the treasure. I also try to be creative, look through archives, and talk to scholars. I have been able to apply for grants and print what is out of print.

I also ask my students to write their own narratives. My students talk to their families and extended families and write their family histories. If stories are not recorded and written down, they may be lost. If language is not recorded, it may be lost. Songs, riddles, nursery rhymes, games, jokes—all of these we work to capture.

Even the most successful teachers should critically consider their positions each year. Sometimes "success" as an educator can make us (teachers) complacent, lazy, or indifferent to the world around us. As educators, we must be the conduits in which students receive critical information about the world, in which they begin to examine themselves and their own communities. If we are not considering the role we play and the success of our own work, then students may likewise become lazy about their own roles and places in society. Education is all about learning and growing. A recent series of events made me reconsider my own position at the school where I teach. I had to decide if I belong, if I should stay, if I am helping or harming the students by filling my teaching position or if another might be better qualified. Ultimately, I believe that I am doing more good than harm.

I know the Zuni culture, like the cultures of all Native communities, is precious, like a precious metal, a precious stone, or a special gift. Within the Zuni Tribe, the culture may not be hidden, or secret, but it *is* sacred. If I don't recognize such cultural gifts as sacred, if there is a possibility that I might misuse such gifts, or even if I don't appreciate them for what they are, then they are best to be kept and treasured by those who value them. If I cannot understand the full answer to my questions if it not my place to understand, or if I cannot benefit from it, then I would rather be told that they cannot share such knowledge; however, I can acknowledge and respect the Zuni culture and appreciate the important role I play as an out-sider in this community, teaching students whose culture is at the heart of almost every aspect of this community.

Part 3

Conclusion

Lessons Learned

Conclusion

Marjori Krebs and Cheryl A. Torrez

We are confident you enjoyed hearing the voices of our authors as they shared their stories. In conclusion, we share the authors' responses when asked to give one word to describe their ZETAC experience. They responded with the following: *incredible, exciting, worthwhile, motivating, legacy, conductive (we all have the ability to transfer positive teaching and learning), fantastic, and empowerment.* As editors we would add our two words also: *inspiring* and *transformative.* We hope you experienced all of this and more as you read this book.

Index

For Product Safety Concerns and Information please contact our EU
representative GPSR@taylorandfrancis.com Taylor & Francis Verlag GmbH,
Kaufingerstraße 24, 80331 München, Germany

Printed and bound by CPI Group (UK) Ltd, Croydon, CR0 4YY
11/04/2025
01844008-0009